Carole Lombard
The Hoosier Tornado

*The stunning beauty of a classic comic actress in
her watershed film* My Man Godfrey *(1936).*

INDIANA BIOGRAPHY SERIES

Carole Lombard
The Hoosier Tornado

WES D. GEHRING

GENERAL EDITORS
RAY E. BOOMHOWER, KATHLEEN M. BREEN, AND PAULA J. CORPUZ

INDIANA HISTORICAL SOCIETY PRESS
INDIANAPOLIS 2003

This book is a publication of the
Indiana Historical Society Press
450 West Ohio Street
Indianapolis, Indiana 46202-3269 USA
www.indianahistory.org
Telephone orders 1-800-447-1830
Fax orders 317-234-0562
Orders by E-mail shop.indianahistory.org

Library of Congress Cataloging-in-Publication Data
Gehring, Wes D.
    Carole Lombard, the Hoosier tornado / Wes D. Gehring.
        p. cm. — (Indiana biography series)
    "Lombard filmography" —P.
    Includes bibliographical references and index.
    ISBN 0-87195-167-3 (alk. paper)
        1. Lombard, Carole, 1908–1942. 2. Motion picture actors and actress-
    es—United States—Biography. I. Title. II. Series.

PN2287.L625G44 2003
791.43'028'092—dc21
[B]   2003041748

Printed in Canada

To Sarah and Emily
and my parents

Carole Lombard:
The "Screwball Girl"

Screwball comedy is essentially about
The crazy rich girl next door
And the comic antihero boy
Who doesn't love her . . . at first.

And though there are several
Recipes available to create
This fruitcake of a genre,
All require lots of mixed nuts.

For best results, add one
Zany heiress to the world
Of some mild-mannered male,
Unaware of his own unhappiness.

Then sprinkle lightly with comic
Character actors, childlike pets,
And oodles of decadent playtime
In the most la-de-da of settings.

Stand back as the ingredients start
To bubble, noting how the male's goose
Is cooked as the screwball heroine
Wears him out with her wackiness.

Properly prepared, this comedy dish
Has served audiences endlessly since
The 1930s, Hollywood's version of the loaves
And the fishes, in 35mm topsyturvydom.

                                        —Wes D. Gehring

An earlier version of this poem first appeared in
Literature/Film Quarterly 10, no. 4 (1982).

TABLE OF CONTENTS

Mainstream Audiences and the Application of Film Theory: The Case of Carole Lombard

Scott Robert Olson

DOES A MAINSTREAM AUDIENCE APPLY FILM THEORY TO A MOVIE it watches? An audience makes sense of the movie-going experience by placing a film into a genre that renders it intelligible and contextual. It's helpful for an audience to know that the movie it's watching is a western or a romantic comedy or a horror film. To get to that understanding, an audience does indeed apply a kind of theory to its experience. What the mainstream audience has is a kind of provisional theory, a rule of thumb that fits most movie watching, but one that is organized quite differently than the ones used by film theorists.

Consequently, a mainstream audience does not apply genre theory the way a film scholar does. A film scholar tends to focus on genre as a variation of auteur theory, as if the only contributions made to the establishment and evolution of each film genre had been made by the directors of those films. That line of reasoning, for example, equates the western with John Ford, and not without justification. But the formula is too simple and therein is its flaw: the auteur approach to genre assumes that the rules of genre come from the style of the directors who make movies within it, and nowhere else. Not only that, but using the auteur theory to explain genre is an odd confluence of antithetical approaches, a scholarly affectation that does not correspond to the commonsensical way audiences really watch movies. The popular audience, perhaps more in tune with what the movies are actually doing, tends to equate genres with performers, with movie stars, not directors. Thus, the mainstream audience equates westerns with John Wayne, not John Ford.

The best example of this populist application of genre theory has to be Carole Lombard. Most members of the audience for screwball comedies equated screwballs with Lombard. She did as much to define the genre as any director, defining its theme, wit, pacing, look, and vocal style. Her mix of toughness, vulnerability, zaniness, and great beauty has found little parallel in the other leading ladies of screwball or romantic comedies. No other actress came to be so associated with a particular comedic form, and no genre came to place a single star so firmly in the firmament. Lombard's movies often toyed with the star-firmament symbiosis she embodied. For example, the emcee at the Casino Moderne in the film *Nothing Sacred* introduces Lombard's small-town character Hazel Flagg to a crowded theater with the exuberant announcement: "I humbly invite her now to take her place alongside all the great heroines of history." This is a proclamation that motion picture audiences then and now were happy to endorse, and one that contributed to the way they understood genre.

Audiences loved Lombard because she promised them laughs and always delivered them. In *Hands Across the Table*, Macklyn's butler tells Lombard's character Regi, "I haven't heard him laugh in a long time." Regi responds, "He's got a few laughs coming to him." So did we, and Lombard made good on the promise. Her character took the snappy banter of the scripts to a new level that belonged only to her and the genre. It worked every time, in spite or even because of her character's blithe ignorance of her comedic effect on her surroundings. Consequently, Regi has no idea that there's anything funny about stopping Manhattan traffic dead in its tracks while she searches for a quarter in the middle of the street to see if it landed heads or tails, or that it landed on its side is anything but deadly serious. Lombard's Irene in *My Man Godfrey* said, "I wish I had a sense of humor, but I can never think of the right thing to say until everybody's gone home." The mainstream audience was still laughing after it went home.

Lombard's life was itself like a motion picture, which is what makes her story such a rich vein for biography. Unfortunately, her story turned out not to be a comedy, but another case of the clown amidst tears. Everyone in *Nothing Sacred* believes that Hazel Flagg is dying of a terminal illness, and everyone around her sobs—everyone except us, of course, because we are already in on the joke. In the end, though, audiences were sobbing, too, because Lombard's life proved to be every bit as short as the life Hazel seemed to be living. Because the genre so belonged to her, she seems to have taken the screwball comedy with her when she died.

Wes Gehring's book is the first biography of Lombard in a long time. Her life is a fascinating and archetypal one. The story has it all and seems like a pitch for a depression-era melodrama. It's a small-town-kid makes good story, from Lombard's birth in Indiana to her childhood in California and then her success in the motion picture business. It's a star-is-born story, with Lombard in the heart of the action at Mack Sennett, Pathé, and Paramount as motion picture comedy was defining itself. It's a romance, with the best leading man central casting could have conceived of: Clark Gable. And, of course, on the outskirts of Las Vegas, too soon, just as she seemed to be breaking free from the genre we continue to equate her with, the story becomes a tragedy. Her life was the stuff of movies, and it makes for a fascinating story as only Gehring can tell it.

So, it seems that the mainstream audience does indeed apply theory to the movie-going experience. The Lombard case is one of the best examples: the consolidation of a genre without an auteur, or perhaps even the star as auteur. Either way, Gehring's book indicates that the mainstream audience knows how to choose its movies and movie stars well. Reading this book, you'll be reminded of what Carole Lombard meant to film comedy, the way she defined audience expectations for what the genre was supposed to be as the introduction of film sound meant the era of silent gags was over. She was, and is, the benchmark. Her character in *Hands Across the Table* asks, "Do you dream? You should—you meet a better class of people!" Movies are the stuff that dreams are made of, of course. Lombard made a better class of movie, and her films still seem like a sweet dream.

Scott Robert Olson is dean of the college of communications, information, and media and professor of communication studies at Ball State University, Muncie, Indiana. Olson's most recent book is Hollywood Planet: Global Media and the Competitive Advantage of Narrative Transparency *(1999). He has published numerous articles about film and television in* The Journal of Communications, The Journal of Film and Video, *and* Critical Studies in Media Communication. *In 2001 Olson was coauthor with Beverly Pitts and Phil Repp of* iCommunication: The Media Design Initiative, *a $20 million project on digital media funded by The Lilly Endowment.*

*"You haven't seen enough movies. All of life's
riddles are answered in the movies."*
—DAVIS (STEVE MARTIN) IN *GRAND CANYON* (1991)

MY FAMILY HAS ALWAYS BEEN FASCINATED BY FUNNY MOVIES.
Screen comedians were central to my upbringing. But while
laughter ruled, there was minimal analysis. Consequently,
most of my adult life has been spent exploring a youth filtered
through film. Like the central character in Walker Percy's celebrated novel, *The Moviegoer*, who and what I am is forever
intertwined with film.[1] Thus, my favorite pieces of time are
not just memories; they are *movie* memories. For example,
images of a beloved grandfather are forever attached to his
tears of laughter over Laurel and Hardy's inspired attempts
to get a piano up an endless flight of stairs in *The Music Box*
(1932). My favorite early memory of my father is tied to his
chuckling enjoyment of W. C. Fields's segment in *If I Had a
Million* (1932), in which the comedian directs an army of
Model-T Fords into comic collisions with assorted road hogs.

Of the dozen and a half books I have devoted to comedy
criticism and biographies of laugh makers, this Carole

Lombard book is a special case. She is a defining presence in my favorite genre—screwball comedy. And during her short (1908–1942), intense life, this was America's favorite type of comedy, too. No less a pivotal period publication than *Life* magazine christened her the "Screwball Girl" in a high profile 1938 cover story.[2] Fittingly, images of her signature roles in the genre were very much a part of my childhood, especially her zany heiress in *My Man Godfrey* (1936). The message in the merriment, the life lesson if you will, was that the irrational mind—crazy Carole—stood a much better chance of surviving in the equally irrational modern world. Just as most vaccines carry a trace of the disease, Lombard's screwball comedy was prescribing a dose of daffiness to get through what seems a less than rational real world. (Years before I became familiar with the pioneering comic antiheroic writing of James Thurber and Robert Benchley, the screwball realm of Lombard had prepared me for their breakthrough in American humor.)

Lombard's screwball moniker, however, was just one of several Carole catchphrases that caught my attention as a young film enthusiast. Her high-octane heartland energy level was wonderfully captured in her nickname "The Hoosier Tornado." And her unusual mix of heavenly beauty and tendency to swear like a sailor resulted in the description "The Profane Angel." But when it came to Lombard, just about everyone was a potential fan. This was especially brought home to me recently while reading writer-director Cameron Crowe's *Conversations with Wilder*. In the course of an engaging portrait of another Hollywood comedy legend, writer-director Billy Wilder, this contemporary of Lombard is asked if he regretted not having worked with any performer. Without missing a beat, Wilder responded, "There was an actress married to Clark Gable . . . Carole Lombard. That was an actress I liked very much. I wanted to work with her . . . and I never even met her."[3]

What makes the response interesting, besides the quickness of the reply, is the change in tone. Wilder, like so many of his movies, is entertainingly cynical about most subjects. It was no accident that his films were often a showcase for dark comedy, such as *Some Like It Hot* (1959), which the American Film Institute picked as the funniest film ever made. Consequently, it is startling to have the Wilder interview turn briefly sentimental when the "what if" subject of Lombard comes up. But that is the power of this free-spirited personality, even after all these years.

Lombard has even changed my take on film critic Molly Haskell's haunting description of the power of the movies—providing "a catharsis for feelings and memories that have been lost, distorted, repressed by time. . . . Movies, our collective unconscious, give us back our pasts, plunge us into the wellspring of feeling with images as vivid and artfully disguised as dreams."[4] While I fully embrace this metaphorical time machine to one's personal past (via the movies), film as a "collective unconscious" only tells part of the story. The vivid film persona created by Lombard in a host of comedies lives on today in the public's collective conscious. Her screwball heroine is as significant for modern audiences as yesteryear's more traditional literary figures. Indeed, the pivotal personae (characters) of cinema history now undoubtedly exert *more* influence on the contemporary audience. (Interestingly, however, Lombard is also a sometimes presence in contemporary fiction, too. See especially Rebecca Wells's critically acclaimed best-selling 1996 novel *Divine Secrets of the Ya-Ya Sisterhood*, where Lombard and Clark Gable are an idealized Hollywood couple.)[5]

This study was immeasurably enriched by both the New York Public Library's Performing Arts Library at Lincoln Center, and the Margaret Herrick Library of the Academy of Motion Picture Arts and Sciences, Beverly Hills, California. During the 1930s heyday of Lombard's career, the most insightfully expansive critiques of her films came from the numerous New York City daily newspapers. These archives were a valuable resource for Lombard reviews, as well as the microfilm holdings of the main branch of the New York Public Library at Fifth Avenue and Forty-second Street.

Numerous people helped make this project a reality. My former department chairperson, "Dr. Joe" Misiewicz, assisted by facilitating university financial help, as did Ball State University provost Warren C. Vander Hill, and college of communication, information, and media dean Scott Robert Olson, who also wrote the foreword.

Ball State professor and film historian Conrad Lane provided invaluable advice in the preparation of the manuscript, as well as logging copyedit time (along with Janet Warrner). Ball State professor and Indiana historian David Smith was also a helpful adviser. The computer preparation of the manuscript was done by Jean Thurman. Coming back full circle to family, a special thank you is in order for my daughters, Sarah and Emily, and my parents. Their love and support make book projects such as this possible.

A final thank you is in order for Ray E. Boomhower, the managing editor of *Traces of Indiana and Midwestern History*. I am forever grateful to his support of my writing, first in the pages of *Traces*, and now with this biography of Lombard. An accomplished historian himself, he is a valuable catalyst for any writer with an important story to tell.

Charlie Chaplin and Marie Dressler in front of then Assistant Secretary of the Navy Franklin D. Roosevelt. Second row center— Douglas Fairbanks Sr. and Mary Pickford. Liberty Loan Drive in Washington, D.C. (14 April 1918).

*"At first thought, we might say, 'our job is to win a war' . . .
but I am sure it would be closer to the hearts of all of us to say,
'We are fighting a war to assure a peace . . . our kind of peace.'"[1]*

CAROLE LOMBARD, INDIANAPOLIS WAR-BOND RALLY, 15 JANUARY 1942

IN THE DAYS AFTER JAPAN'S SURPRISE ATTACK ON PEARL HARBOR and Germany's subsequent declaration of war on America, President Franklin D. Roosevelt considered the high cost of waging a war both in Asia and Europe. To help fund the war effort, he immediately thought of the hugely successful American war-bond rallies during World War I that were spearheaded by such Hollywood stars as Charlie Chaplin, Douglas Fairbanks Sr., and Mary Pickford. Roosevelt had firsthand knowledge of the rallies because he had joined these performers (and actress Marie Dressler) in a Washington, D.C., Liberty Loan Drive on 14 April 1918 when he was assistant secretary of the navy.[2]

Roosevelt also kept in mind his association with Hollywood in the 1930s, when he frequently called upon movie stars to attend his annual birthday celebrations, which were used as ambitious fund-raisers to battle against infantile paralysis.[3]

Because of these past successes, it was only logical that the president turned to the film capital at the start of the war. Fittingly, the government contacted Metro-Goldwyn-Mayer, whose advertising slogan at that time was "more stars than in the heavens." MGM head Louis B. Mayer suggested that a new war-bond campaign be headed by one of the studio's reigning stars, such as Clark Gable or Mickey Rooney, the two top box-office draws in America for 1941.[4] All things being equal, Rooney seemed the more logical choice. In addition to being the number one box-office attraction for 1941 (as well as 1939 and 1940), he was also a friend of the president, having entertained at the White House during the aforementioned birthday fund-raisers. Plus, Rooney enjoyed performing before a live audience, which was pivotal to a bond campaign's success.

Gable won the honor, however, because presidential adviser Harry Hopkins believed the bond drive should be launched from America's heartland (Gable was originally from Ohio; Rooney had been born in Brooklyn). Roosevelt concurred, adding that Gable's sex appeal would probably sell more bonds than Rooney's youthful enthusiasm. What they had not anticipated was Gable's lack of confidence at appearing before a live audience. He turned Hopkins down, stating, "I'll help you in any way I can, other than personal appearances. But I hate crowds and I don't know how to act when I'm in one. Besides, I'm no salesman."[5]

Gable's wife, film star Carole Lombard, told Hopkins she

would be able to change her husband's mind. Lombard promised Gable she would accompany him and help out. When that did not work, she played a patriotism card, telling him what an honor it was to be asked to kick off the war-bond campaign. But Gable turned the tables on her by answering, "Right, Maw [his nickname for Lombard], consider yourself asked."[6] When it was clear she could not convince her husband otherwise, Lombard accepted Gable's offer, though she was still hopeful he would accompany her.

Roosevelt and Hopkins were both pleased with this new development, feeling that a high-profile female star such as Lombard might sell even more bonds than a man. Moreover, Roosevelt still remembered and greatly appreciated Lombard's 1938 endorsement of both his administration and income tax in general, despite her paying more than 85 percent of her salary in state and federal taxes. ("I have no kicks at all," Lombard had said at the time. "[The] fact is I'm pretty happy about the whole thing. . . . I enjoy this country. I like the parks and the highways and the good schools and everything that this Government does.")[7] Of course, the topper to Lombard's selection was that she was from the heartland state of Indiana. In fact, the Hoosier connection became the official reason given for Lombard's involvement in the project. "The honor of being the first state to have a Defense bond rally on a state-wide basis since the war began was accorded Indiana because the Hoosier state led in Liberty bond sales, on a per capita basis, in the first world war," noted the *Indianapolis News*.[8]

Consistent with this position, it was logical that Lombard would lead the mid-January bond drive back in Indianapolis. The Indiana continuity with World War I was further accented by booking a second famous Hollywood Hoosier to join Lombard in the state capital: Will H. Hays, the former censorship czar of American films who had been in charge of selling Indiana's Liberty Bonds during the previous war. Hoosier pride became a selling point for Lombard. When she spoke at Indianapolis's Cadle Tabernacle the evening of 15 January 1942 (after a full day of patriotic activities), she concluded her speech with these words: "As a Hoosier, I am proud that Indiana led the nation in buying Liberty Bonds in the last war. I want to believe that Indiana will lead every other state again this time—and we will! We won the last war. And, with your help, we will win this war!"[9]

Once Lombard was convinced that Gable would not accompany her, she asked her mother, Elizabeth "Bessie" Peters, to join her on this patriotic adventure. As with several other period screen actresses, Lombard was extremely close to her mother, who often doubled as a best friend and companion. Peters immediately accepted the invitation, with the understanding she would make a brief side trip to their Indiana hometown of Fort Wayne.

To celebrate the trip Lombard outfitted Peters with a new Beverly Hills wardrobe, assuring her she was the sexiest mother in America. Peters kidded back that maybe she would find a Hoosier millionaire in Indianapolis. The two were also

4

William G. Johnson, business representative of the United Brewery and Soft Drink Workers of America, hands Carole Lombard a $3,000 check for war-bond purchases from the union.

accompanied by Otto Winkler, an MGM press agent and a friend of Gable and Lombard. (Winkler and Peters had also been the only Hollywood guests at Gable and Lombard's 1939 secret getaway wedding.) Though Lombard was not associated with MGM (it was Gable's home studio), she was acting on the request of a husband who was also the head of the actors' division of the Hollywood Victory Committee. Under these circumstances, it was natural policy for the studio to provide a press agent as a buffer—not that Lombard ever needed a buffer at any time in her life.

The trio of Lombard, Peters, and Winkler left Hollywood aboard the City of Los Angeles train on Monday, 12 January 1942. A short stop in Salt Lake City enabled Lombard to test her bond-selling skills, as a crowd had gathered in anticipation of her Chicago-bound train. Always a passionate and patriotic person, she easily took to this whistle-stop opportunity to hone her speaking skills, becoming a flag-waving hit. Upon reaching Chicago on 14 January, Lombard discussed her onetime fear of public speaking, just prior to a WGN radio broadcast. But what comes through in her words is a pep talk-like enthusiasm for defense and the Hollywood Victory Committee: "Years ago I used to be afraid to make speeches, but when you've got bonds to sell, and the country the way it is [patriotically involved], you go right ahead. [It's the] least you can do. . . . Well, it's terrific. This is the first unity Hollywood ever had. We're to have from 10 to 25 [war-bond] shows on the road at one time. . . . From now on it's sell a bond, sell a bond, sell a bond. You finish a picture and before you get off the [studio] lot, it's [waving a commanding finger] 'Pittsburgh by 4 o'clock [for a bond rally]' and off you go again. It's terrific!"[10]

Chicago Tribune journalist Marcia Winn affectionately observed of Lombard at the time: "Vivid, gay, she never stopped talking, her comments as colorful as her hat." The actress proved to be gracious as well. Winn noted: "Could she come up [to the *Tribune*]? Of course she could. . . . Speak over W-G-N? Of course. Interviews? Of course. Autographs? Of course."[11]

This whirlwind of words and movement (she paced as she talked) fit Lombard's Hollywood nickname, "The Hoosier Tornado." With an opinion on everything, a fascination with all aspects of filmmaking, and a wicked sense of humor, she might have been a film critic in another age. Indeed, a later description of famed *New Yorker* movie reviewer Pauline Kael, a big fan of Lombard screwball comedies as a young woman, reads like a profile of the actress: "She seemed constantly in motion, and constantly talking and laughing, too, saying so much that one was amazed by how much she also heard. At a screening, she reacted audibly to many things in the movie . . . sometimes panicking nearby moviegoers with a loudly muttered joke."[12]

Kael's own description of the actress was more succinct— "the grinning infectiousness of Carole Lombard."[13] This Hoosier-born entertainer had used that "grinning infectiousness" to get her way since she was a Fort Wayne six year old racing her friends to a top-of-the stairs bedroom at the family home on Rockhill Street. Lombard brought a missionary zeal to whatever she undertook, whether learning to box as a child or ultimately selling war bonds.

Although always devoted to her country, Lombard had during the 1930s displayed isolationist tendencies, even threatening to chain Gable to a barn door if he attempted to enlist.[14] Everything changed with the Japanese attack on Pearl Harbor. Though she still believed "women probably could have done a better job of ruling the world," when she was invited to Indianapolis to sell defense bonds she whooped as only Lombard could whoop, and headed east.[15] ("She could sell anything" was Gable's take on the subject.)

Lombard and Winkler stayed in Chicago for several hours, doing bond-related publicity, while Peters went on by train for a brief stopover in Fort Wayne. Lombard biographer Larry Swindell has the actress and agent then flying to Indianapolis and reconnecting with Peters on Thursday, 15 January, when the latter arrived by train.[16] Period accounts, however, have the trio arriving together by rail early Thursday afternoon, where they were met at Union Station by Indianapolis mayor Reginald H. Sullivan and other dignitaries.[17] Thus, Lombard and Winkler must have stayed over in Chicago Wednesday night and then taken an Indianapolis-bound train the following morning. Somewhere along the way Peters must have joined them.

Regardless, Lombard, who likened her sales-pitch style to a "barker at a carnival," had an overbooked Thursday.[18] Her first official act was a two o'clock flag-raising ceremony at the Indiana statehouse, where Gov. Henry F. Schricker introduced her as "the little Hoosier girl who made good in Hollywood."[19] The actress was the last of several speakers on a cold, windy Indiana winter day. She concluded her short, impassioned speech with the dramatic direction, "Heads up, hands up, America! Let's give a cheer that will be heard in Tokyo and Berlin!"[20] The crowd went wild, with "one voice above the others calling, 'Carole, the victory girl,' as she made the victory sign with her fingers against the background of the Stars and Stripes."[21]

The aforementioned "heads up" conclusion to Lombard's speech might have been inspired by Chaplin's then famous war-related address that closed *The Great Dictator* (1940), where he encourages the heroine to "Look up, Hannah, look up [and have faith]!" Though many period movie critics faulted Chaplin for stepping out of character to deliver it, the speech was popular with the public, and the comedian was frequently asked to reprise the address. Given that Chaplin had the highest profile of any artist in prewar Hollywood, it makes sense that Lombard might have been influenced by the film, especially as the high point of her teen years was a 1924 screen test for the comedian's *Gold Rush* (1925). Regardless of its source, the close of Lombard's speech displayed the passion the actress brought to every activity. She was most articulate on this subject in a 1938

Charlie Chaplin's dark comedy send-up of Hitler
in The Great Dictator *(1940).*

Motion Picture magazine article, telling an interviewer, "I'm intensely interested in and enthusiastic about everything I do, *everything.* No matter what it is I'm doing ... I give it all I've got and I love it. . . . If I don't love what I'm doing I don't do it."[22]

The flag-raising ceremony outside the statehouse lasted until shortly after half past two, then Lombard and the other dignitaries moved inside to the rotunda for a furious hour of bond sales. With a long line already formed since early morning, the actress had her work cut out for her. Patriotic buyers received a bond receipt bearing her picture and autograph, which she signed "Carole Lombard Gable." The actress also had a smile and a ready quip for every customer, such as the man who asked, "Where's Clark?" "Oh, he's home working," Lombard replied. "Someone in the family has to work, you know."[23] She was surprised only that it had been a man who first asked about her matinee-idol husband. Lombard gave a "ringing laugh" when a mother with a sleeping baby told the actress that the child, for whom she was buying the war bond, was Carole's namesake. With that, the actress took time to pat the baby gently and say, "Why, bless her heart."[24] (Fittingly, Lombard's most famous namesake is comedienne Carol Burnett, born in 1933.)

The original sales goal for the rotunda rally had been $500,000, though Schricker hoped to reach $1 million. But when Lombard asked for a total after almost an hour of steady trade, she was pleased to discover sales already were well above $1 million. "'We'll make it two,' she laughed, and turned back to business."[25] Amazingly, when the final figures were tabulated later in the day, her bond sales had done just that. This phenomenal tally was not limited to just a "meet the movie star" mentality. Lombard knew sales. She limited autographs to the red, white, and blue bond receipts. The actress also directed a legion of salesgirls with entertainingly knowing tips, such as, "The fellow in the brown suit will go five hundred [dollars for a bond]—kiss his bald head and tell him it's from me!"[26] For a time Lombard even mounted a table both to be seen and to spy additional customers.

At half past three Lombard went briefly to her hotel (Indianapolis's Claypool) to raise a large flag to the top of a thirty-six-foot staff in the lobby. This action officially opened recruiting booths there for the army, navy, and marines. A brief stop in her hotel suite revealed dozens of roses sent by Gable. The actress explained to impressed visitors that it was their custom, when apart, to bombard the traveling partner with large quantities of the flower.

Lombard was then almost immediately whisked away to the governor's mansion for a tea and reception both for the actress and the women members of the Indiana Defense Savings staff. Press coverage revealed that "so irresistible was the spell cast by Miss Carole Lombard . . . that, though it was supposed to be a completely social affair, guests began taking orders for defense bonds from each other."[27] This was no small accomplishment given that everyone was a member of the Defense Savings staff! But maybe part of this success came from Lombard's brief opening comments at the tea, "Ladies, you are doing a magnificent job." Journalist Florence Webster Long later reported, "Never did a public speech make more of a hit than her seven-word classic."[28] Of course, Lombard

*Five-year-old Indianapolis youth Melvin Dennis Loeb
receives a handshake from Lombard for his purchase
of a twenty-five dollar war bond (15 January 1942).*

seldom limited herself to such brief statements. For example, when asked at the same tea what women do best to help win the war, she responded: "I think morale work is the most important just now. That is, until a regular women's army has been organized, as we've been promised it will be. I think it's particularly important for women to . . . concentrate on taking care of their own homes and their own families the very best they can."[29]

That evening Lombard was a featured speaker at the Cadle Tabernacle. More than twelve thousand Hoosiers turned out for a war rally that began at seven o'clock with patriotic and popular music by bands from both Indiana University and Purdue University. In Lombard's speech, she movingly observed that everybody in the country knew what the war was going to cost. "But the peace it will bring is priceless," she said. "We know what an enormous task lies ahead. . . . [But] as Americans, we have the rare privilege of deciding for ourselves the direction we are to take. We have made that decision."[30]

Again there was an impressive audience response, which she then topped by leading the crowd in a rousing rendition of the national anthem. It was the perfect conclusion to a perfect Lombard day. As one Hoosier journalist observed, "Carole Lombard never scored a greater success on the screen than in her latest role as saleswoman for Uncle Sam."[31] The actress herself said, "I have never been entertained more perfectly than today in Indiana. And I've never been so convinced that the American people are really united in this crisis."[32]

With Lombard's Hoosier bond-sales assignment at a close, she now put all of her sizable energy toward getting back to her Hollywood home and Gable, who had encouraged her to return as soon as possible. The prearranged return schedule had the trio of Lombard, Peters, and Winkler leaving Indianapolis for California by train on Saturday, 17 January. But Lombard was never a prearranged sort of woman. Plus, as the actress explained to *Life* magazine photographer Myron Davis shortly after making flight arrangements, she could not handle three more days on a "choo-choo train."[33]

Lombard was used to getting her way, but the decision to fly back was strongly challenged by both of her traveling companions. First, Winkler was responsible to the government for getting the actress on a train. Officials had concerns about putting bond talent on planes—because of the chance of both general mishaps and war-related sabotage. Second, Lombard's mother was deathly afraid of flying. Third, Peters was a numerologist and all the signs for this flight were bad, she warned. In numerology, three is a hard-luck number. The trio's DC-3 plane would be Flight 3 from New York. They were a party of three. And Lombard was thirty-three years and three months old.[34] Not surprisingly, Peters put up a stiff fight, as did Winkler. Although he was no numerologist, he wanted to follow the government directive and at the same time get some sleep—Flight 3 was scheduled to leave Indianapolis shortly after four in the morning on Friday, 16 January. Ultimately, the stocky, well-liked press agent served as a sort of referee between the dueling daughter and mother. With no agreement reached, he suggested a coin flip. The actress won.

Period accounts reveal, however, that the argument continued at the Indianapolis airport. Numerous witnesses overheard Peters continue to warn her daughter, "Carole, we musn't take that plane."[35] Winkler again used the rest-routine request, noting there were no sleeping accommodations and the flight would take seventeen hours. But Lombard said, "I'll curl up and take a pill and pff I'll be asleep."[36] Even the aforementioned *Life* photographer gently entered the dispute in support of Winkler, telling the actress she looked tired. Lombard dismissed his concern with a wave of her hand and the comment, "When I get home, I'll flop in bed and sleep for twelve hours."[37]

Sadly, that never happened. Early Friday evening, shortly after refueling at Las Vegas, the plane carrying Lombard, Peters, Winkler, and nineteen others crashed in the Spring Mountains. There were no survivors. America was stunned. Among the scores of tributes that followed her shocking death, Roosevelt's telegram to Gable was the most movingly articulate: "Mrs. Roosevelt and I are deeply distressed. Carole was our friend, our guest in happier days. She brought great joy to all who knew her and to the millions who knew her only as a great artist. She gave unselfishly of her time and talent to serve her Government in peace and war. She loved her country. She is and always will be a star, one we shall never forget nor cease to be grateful to."[38]

Of the many comments made by Hollywood friends, most were along the lines of a stunned Walter Pidgeon: "I am too shocked to express anything but the deepest grief." But there were two memorable exceptions. Errol Flynn stated a poignant and almost poetic sense of loss: "Carole Lombard's tragic death means that something of gaiety and beauty have been taken from the world at a time they are needed most." James Cagney honored her as a fallen war hero. "Carole Lombard died doing her job for her country. Every one of us is proud of her," said the actor.[39]

In the days and weeks that followed Lombard's death, Cagney's patriotic perspective dominated, as in the *New York Herald-Tribune*'s statement, "For all her identity with the somewhat unreal goings-on of celluloid comedy, she was a thoroughgoing patriot."[40] The *Washington Times-Herald* opined, "It must be no small consolation for Clark Gable that she gave her life for her country."[41]

As Hollywood linked Lombard's high-energy work ethic to her Indiana background, calling her "The Hoosier Tornado," the actress's patriotic egalitarian nature was associated with a populism inherent to the nineteenth state. For example, a syndicated Hollywood article shortly after her death explained the grief felt by her blue-collar film friends: "Miss Lombard not only was loved but respected as a straight-shooter. Every grip [set mover], every property boy, every commissary waitress adored her for she had the common touch, the common speech and never for a minute forgot they were fellow workers."[42] Thus, the movie star simply called "Pete" by her working-class friends and "Maw" by her husband, in death found the name *patriot*.

1

The Early Years

*"You have a wonderful sense of humor. I wish I had
a sense of humor, but I can never think of the right thing to say
until everybody's gone home."*

CAROLE LOMBARD TO WILLIAM POWELL IN *MY MAN GODFREY* (1936)

FILM ACTRESS CAROLE LOMBARD, CHRISTENED THE "SCREWBALL
girl" by *Life* magazine in 1938, was born Jane Alice Peters on
6 October 1908. (For the sake of familiarity and simplicity, she
will be referred to by her screen name throughout this work.)
Home was an impressive two-story brick-and-wood-frame
structure at 704 Rockhill Street in Fort Wayne, Indiana. Her
parents, Frederic Peters and Elizabeth "Bessie" Knight Peters,
were both from upper-middle-class backgrounds. Indeed,
Carole's early Indiana years could be labeled privileged. The
Peters and Knights were from Fort Wayne's "best" families; the
Knights represented "old money," which included diversified
holdings anchored in East Coast banking concerns. Charles
Knight, Bessie's father, found a managerial position for his son-
in-law in one of the family's businesses, a pioneering washing-
machine concern called the Horton Company.

Carole was the youngest of three children. Frederic Peters
Jr. was born in 1902, followed by a second son, Stuart, in 1906.

Consistent with the screwball movie genre so closely identified with her name, Lombard's Hoosier years had many of the earmarks of this type of film: a matriarchal household, a well-to-do setting, and a free-spirited tomboy daughter who invariably got her way. Appropriately for a future film star, young Lombard's most cherished pastime was movie night—Fridays at the old Colonial Theatre, located on the corner of Calhoun Street and Washington Boulevard in downtown Fort Wayne. Her cinema favorites were the action serials of Kathlyn Williams and Pearl White. Childhood friend Robert Baral later revealed that Friday's movie outing dictated Saturday's play activities; the future actress loved to re-create her favorite movie scenes.[1]

It was unusual at that time for "better" families to patronize this nascent art form. This period lack of respect for the movies is best chronicled by Lombard contemporary, and later celebrated film critic, James Agee. In his posthumous, Pulitzer prize–winning novel, *A Death in the Family*, which was loosely based on his childhood, a boy bonds with his father over the controversial comedy of a then new comedian named Charlie Chaplin. This might just have been the Lombard story, though the girl's movie companion was her mother, Bessie, who once had acting aspirations and enjoyed this new medium.

When Carole was not immersed in the movies, her passion was sports. With two older brothers and a neighborhood largely composed of boys, she tagged along with Frederic

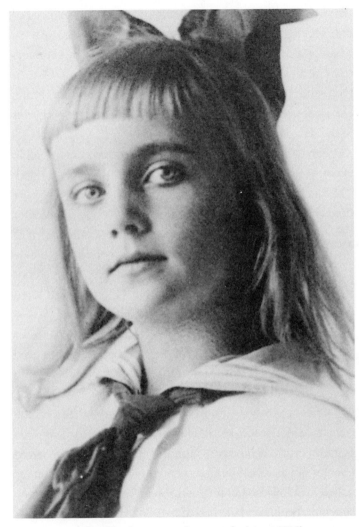

ALLEN COUNTY–FORT WAYNE HISTORICAL SOCIETY

Lombard at approximately age eight (circa 1916).

(known as Fritz) and Stuart, whether they wanted her along or not. Although she excelled at every sport, Carole was especially adept at baseball and swimming, made easier by summers spent at the family cottage on Sylvan Lake at Rome City. In high school she became a track-and-field star, and later during her Hollywood years she won acclaim as the best tennis player in the film community.

Sports and movies notwithstanding, the most memorable event in Carole's Fort Wayne childhood was the 1913 flood. The Peters home, though on high ground, stands very near the Saint Marys River (with a nearby bridge now named after the actress). The family residence became a command post for the area, with Bessie, greatly assisted by having the only phone in the area, orchestrating relief workers. Through her efforts, she became a hero both to her family (the children were meant to feel like important assistants) and to the community. While not a dangerous situation, the fear of further flooding sometimes produced a sort of comedy chaos, as tired people performed a million and one tasks, from gathering extra bedding to brewing oceans of coffee.

Of course, when this overwrought panic was past, it took upon a more comic tone. Coincidentally, a Lombard comedy contemporary, celebrated humorist James Thurber, wrote about a similar situation that occurred at the same time in his native Columbus, Ohio. People had panicked when they thought the local dam had burst. Thurber kiddingly later observed, "The fact that we were all as safe as kittens under a cookstove did not, however, assuage in the least the fine despair and the grotesque desperation which seized upon the residents of the East Side."[2]

There is no record as to Bessie's most exciting experience prior to the 1913 flood, but to anyone outside the family a case could be made for calling this adventure a milestone in her Indiana life, just as it was for her daughter, because the following year she permanently transplanted herself and all three children to Los Angeles. Ostensibly, this was merely to be an extended vacation for Bessie. But if this were true, why would she pull her children out of school to accompany her? The real explanation reveals a family tragedy that encouraged Lombard's mother to embrace what was once called a "Victorian divorce" (when a married couple maintains separate, often distant, residences).

The catalyst for the move originated with an industrial accident that nearly took Peters's life shortly before his marriage to Bessie. He suffered a crippling leg injury that left him with a lifelong impairment. Over time, however, this would be the least of his worries. A more debilitating side effect of the accident was periodic mood-altering headaches that became both more frequent and more frightening during the course of his marriage. While the public image for this Fort Wayne family was forever happy and even mildly screwball, the reality was that the mounting stress eventually forced Bessie to move to southern California.

It bears noting that years later, after Lombard's career-

A wistful Lombard in a scene from My Man Godfrey *(1936, with William Powell and Gail Patrick in the background).*

defining role in the classic film *My Man Godfrey*, the actress credited her Oscar-nominated performance to an unwritten sense of tragedy that she associated with the character. Though Lombard never fully articulated just what that tragic dimension was, it is easy to imagine she was thinking of her own sometimes screwball family and the sad fate of her father. Lombard's dad had died in 1935, the year prior to making *My Man Godfrey*.

Regardless of the actress's inspiration for this later role, Lombard's initial concern about accompanying her mother and brothers on this California vacation was that it would disrupt her viewing of those all-important movie serials at the local theater. But once caught up in the anticipation of a temporary holiday from school and the excitement of a trip to the then seemingly distant and exotic southern California, this little girl was hardly a reluctant traveler.

The family's first Los Angeles residence was at an apartment complex called the Alvarado Terrace on Hoover Street, near Venice Boulevard. First-grader Carole attended Hoover Elementary school with her brother Stuart, while Bessie's oldest child, Fritz, went to junior high. The family's lifestyle was not as luxurious as in Fort Wayne, but they were comfortable. Most importantly, the regular support checks from Bessie's husband (more evidence that a permanent separation had been planned all along) freed her from the need to work.

The free spiritedness later associated with Lombard was first a hallmark of her mother, who blossomed in the pluralist society that was southern California. For example, Bessie became involved in both numerology and the Baha'i faith, a religion founded in Persia in the nineteenth century. Never a fan of organized religion, Bessie became attracted to the faith's minimal dogma. Moreover, as a pioneering feminist, she was drawn to the emphasis this faith placed upon the equality of men and women. This tenet of gender equality became a central precept in the rearing of her daughter.[3]

Of course, in the Peters household, equality for the future actress meant merely holding her own with her older

WES D. GEHRING

Lombard relaxes on a 1937 movie set.

brothers. In her later high-profile Hollywood years, Lombard frequently preached female superiority to anyone who cared to listen. For example, in a 1937 *Photoplay* article titled "Carole Lombard Tells: 'How I Live by a Man's Code,'" she observed that women held an advantage in business. "Men are so secure in their belief that they are supreme in business that they are often caught napping by alert women," she said. "Man thinks he's dealing with an inferior brain when it comes to a woman, and that makes him a sucker."[4]

Gender conflict for the young Lombard centered upon her ongoing interest in sports. One of her earliest profilers noted, "During . . . grammar school days, she would scream with rage if the boys refused to let her participate in their sports."[5] Though she continued to enjoy baseball, her early California years introduced the transplanted Hoosier to soccer and tennis. Appropriately enough for a screen-obsessed child residing in the budding film capital of the world, Lombard continued to play at mimicking the movies.

Strangely enough, her interest in sports was the catalyst for her first movie break. Bessie and her family were visiting friends when twelve-year-old Carole and fourteen-year-old Stuart joined a nearby pickup baseball game. In a twist befitting a Hollywood screenplay, the hard-playing Lombard was spotted by screen director Allan Dwan, a filmmaker best known today for his swashbuckling collaborations with Douglas Fairbanks Sr. In an interview conducted by film historian and director Peter Bogdanovich, Dwan remembered

Lombard as "a cute-looking little tomboy . . . out there knocking hell out of the other kids, playing better baseball than they were. And I needed someone of her type for this picture."[6]

The movie in question was a minor melodrama titled *A Perfect Crime* (1921). The part of the male lead's kid sister was an ideal match for Lombard, if mother and daughter agreed. They *jumped* at the chance. While never a pushy stage parent, Bessie had always encouraged her daughter's acting aspirations, enrolling Carole in a once-a-week drama class even before being discovered by Dwan. Although the role was a small part and Lombard was only on the set for two days, she enjoyed the experience immensely.

One Lombard biographer has suggested that her part in the movie was actually an outgrowth of Bessie's acquaintanceship with the film's Indianapolis-born star—Monte Blue.[7] But this seems unlikely, given Dwan's comments to Bogdanovich. Moreover, Dwan was famous for discovering child performers. In addition to Lombard, his finds included Natalie Wood and Ida Lupino. Plus, Dwan's brief description of Lombard's debut reveals a filmmaker at home with directing young talent. He noted that Lombard "ate it [the part] up. Of course, it was silent. If we'd given her lines to remember, she'd probably have been terrified, but we always made kids feel they were playing and not working. When you give them words to learn, it becomes an ordeal."[8]

This is not to deny, however, that there was something of a Hoosier colony in Hollywood. But it would affect Lombard more in later years. For example, the popular screen cowboy Buck Jones was from Vincennes, Indiana, and made a point of working with transplanted Hoosiers. Thus, Lombard eventually performed in three of his low-budget westerns—*Gold and the Girl, Hearts and Spurs,* and *Durand of the Badlands* (all 1925). Jones also gave Lombard her first screen kiss in *Durand of the Badlands.* (Much later he amusingly confessed that she was not only the prettiest woman he had kissed, but also the prettiest he had ever seen!)

These appearances, though, were several years off. Lombard's initial foray into the movies did not lead immediately to additional film work. It was, after all, only a small part in a modest picture that was not broadly distributed. Of course, mother and daughter had had high hopes and Carole attended a few auditions, but nothing more surfaced. Still, southern California constantly provided distractions. About the same time as *A Perfect Crime*, Carole and Stuart were able to receive boxing instructions from none other than Benny Leonard, the former lightweight champion of the world.

This exciting development, mistakenly associated, on occasion, with her discovery by Dwan, was the outgrowth of a family visit to some friends of Bessie's, the Kaufmans. Mr. Kaufman originally had asked the boxer to tutor young Stuart, but the athletic Carole was not to be denied and both children soon found themselves listening attentively with gloved hands at their sides. When they started to spar, however, it was the tomboy who proved to be the natural boxer. When Carole was

Lombard is shown putting her childhood boxing lessons to use in one of her greatest films, Nothing Sacred *(1937, with Fredric March as victim and Walter Connolly looking on).*

not dancing away from Stuart's punches, she was peppering him with baby jabs and hooks. Fittingly, the girl who had been a tough battler since birth was equally at home in the ring.

In addition to being an entertaining incident, it is a pivotal event for three additional reasons. First, it nicely demonstrated the important contacts Bessie had through a wide circle of influential California friends. Second, this Leonard tutorial eventually achieved special distinction when the highlight of one of her later signature films (*Nothing Sacred*, 1937) had her trading punches with Fredric March. Third, the image of Lombard as a feisty fighter ultimately served as an apt metaphor for the actress's gung-ho philosophy of life.

Other than her ongoing propensity to personally re-create scenes from favorite films, Lombard's youth proceeded without any new movie roles. There were, however, certain constants in her life, including the ongoing importance of both her mother and brothers. Their significance was further enhanced by Bessie's tendency to periodically move the family—forever attempting to maximize their fixed income. Consequently, while neighbors and neighborhoods might change, Lombard's best friends were always under her roof. This especially applied to her relationship with Bessie. There was neither the traditional generation gap when Lombard was a teenager, nor the standard power plays when the wanna-be actress became a movie star. Even as the legendary Lombard, if she could not see her mother on almost a daily basis, she called her frequently on the telephone. One reporter noted: "'That Bessie,' she [Lombard] would say, 'is she terrific! Do you adore her? Let's call her up.' She was always calling Bessie up at odd hours, from strange places, for screwy reasons, with a new story or a bit of gossip or a sudden plan."[9]

After their deaths, Lombard's journalist friend Adela Rogers St. Johns wrote about the actress's "unusually close love for her mother." St. Johns was most poignantly insightful when she penned something later seconded by the family: "Someone said to me this morning that it seemed so awful that her mother should have been killed, too. I can't feel that, knowing them. It would have been so awful for the one who was left."[10]

Lombard's brothers represented more rough-and-tumble buddies, with the six years older Fritz doubling as a surrogate father. They taught her the ropes on everything from sports to boys, while Lombard's girlfriends frequently had crushes on the brothers. Of course, the brothers' most famous tutorial for their sister involved teaching her how to swear like a sailor. The catalyst for this was Lombard's frustration as a young adult at conventional ways of warding off overly aggressive suitors. Initially, the brothers balked at her request. But as Fritz later explained, "Sis wouldn't let us off the hook. She'd hit on the idea of discouraging her would-be seducers by swearing at them. . . . So we more or less said all right, you asked for it, and started at the beginning. Just getting started was the only embarrassing part. Soon it became a little game, and we all relaxed and enjoyed it. I remember that Stuart especially couldn't stop laughing."[11]

Lombard was nothing if not thorough when she embraced something new, and what started out as a dating defense eventually became one of her defining Hollywood trademarks. Other than some early pushy dates, most people were seldom put off by the colorful language. In a later interview with the actress's *Nothing Sacred* director, William Wellman, the Oscar-winning filmmaker said, "Lombard *did* say dirty words but not all the time. And when she did say them, for some reason or another, they didn't sound like dirty words. There was a poetic something about her."[12] Obviously, her free-spirited, one-of-the-boys charisma was true on screen and off. Sometimes she might swear for shock, but that was only part of it. More often than not, she used earthy verbiage as a calculated tool to put a conversation with a male on a more relaxed level. Moreover, she often had an inspired knack for using such language in a comic manner. The most celebrated example during her lifetime involved a question as to whether her wealthy banking executive great-grandfather Cheney had helped finance the laying of the first transatlantic cable. He had, but Lombard preferred to say, "No, the only thing Grandpa ever laid was Grandma." (The Criterion Collection DVD of *My Man Godfrey* contains several outtakes of Lombard's colorful response to blowing lines of dialogue.)

Lombard's language makeover was, however, still several years in the future when her 1921 Dwan-directed screen baptism failed to blossom into a career as a child star. Returning to reality meant starting junior high school that fall. After several apartments, the family had graduated to a house, and Carole now had her own room in which to entertain her new friends. The importance of movies was now rivaled by girlfriends dressed as Jazz Age "flappers," dancing, tennis, and boys a distant fourth. School was fine but hardly the highest priority.

Much-honored biographer Frank E. Vandiver once observed that profiling a life "is history made personal."[13] In

Lombard's case, this period connection is best applied to the fact that the 1914 Peters family's move to southern California coincided with the shift of the film industry from New York to the West Coast and the emergence of Hollywood as America's new film capital. The West Coast offered both year-round fair weather and a broad assortment of topography (from the mountains to the seashore) for whatever genre backdrop was needed. Since Lombard later excelled in comedy, one might best document the transition then taking place in American screen comedy. In the years just prior to the Peters family's California relocation, John Bunny was *the* American screen comedian. His Vitagraph Studio was within walking distance of his Brooklyn home. But even prior to his unexpected death in 1915, he was being usurped by newcomer Charlie Chaplin, who started making films for Mack Sennett's California-based Keystone Company in 1914. (Lombard later served a comedy apprenticeship with Sennett.)

While films had been shot in the Los Angeles area as early as 1908, this mid-1910s explosion of quality Hollywood film product, including D. W. Griffith's watershed 1915 film *The Birth of a Nation*, triggered an annual Hollywood migration of potential actors numbering in the tens of thousands. The motion picture industry even started shooting documentaries discouraging the flood of cinema hopefuls. This was the movie-mania environment into which the Peters family had moved. Regardless of the school Carole attended, a sizable segment of her peers' parents were involved in the picture business. Even

WES D. GEHRING

Fat, funny and forgotten—John Bunny was America's first important screen comedian (circa 1915).

if young Lombard had not been fascinated by film, it would have been difficult to avoid catching this cinema fervor.

While Bessie and the children's Indiana exit was not predicated upon getting into the new California film industry, their move did reflect another factor fueling small-town migration to Hollywood and elsewhere. What later critics termed the "revolt from the village" was the literary movement that chronicled a growing dissatisfaction with the limitations and/or biases of small-town America.[14] A pivotal early "revolt from the village" work was midwestern poet Edgar Lee Masters's *Spoon River Anthology* (1915), which was set in a state (Illinois) adjacent to Indiana. Masters's haunting collection of free-verse poems—each one spoken from the grave by a different frustrated individual whose small-town life had been wasted—represented an attack on hypocrisy and its frequent companion, smugness. During the 1920s, novelist Sinclair Lewis brilliantly articulated this revolt mentality in a series of best-sellers starting with *Main Street* (1920) and *Babbitt* (1922). As Lewis scholar Glen A. Love observed, "*Main Street* had announced unequivocally and for all time that the American small town was not the unalloyed friendship village of our [past] mythology."[15]

Bessie never went on record with anything half this hostile about Fort Wayne, maintaining ties with Hoosier friends and family for the rest of her life. That being said, however, Bessie's Indiana years had anticipated the culture-starved life of *Main Street* heroine Carol Kennicott. For example, the friendship between Bessie and actor Blue was an outgrowth of their teenage encounters when she made periodic theater trips to Indianapolis. Such cultural outings helped, but Bessie was well aware of a bigger world beyond the state capital. Thus, while the mood swings of Lombard's father were apparently the catalyst for the move by Bessie and her children, she had had wanderlust in her heart since youth. (Interestingly enough, Lombard's pivotal film, *Nothing Sacred*, had the actress playing a character willing to do anything to exit her small-town home.)

As Carole moved on to Fairfax High School, she often traveled in fast company. Two of her early dating partners were sons of very prominent national figures, newspaper magnate and sometime movie power player William Randolph Hearst and pioneering filmmaker Thomas Ince. Hearst, of course, is now most famous for being the complex figure upon which Orson Welles based *Citizen Kane* (1941), widely acknowledged as being the greatest movie ever made. Though Ince is less well known today, he was one of the most influential figures in the history of cinema. He essentially invented what is now known as the modern producer, from developing detailed shooting scripts to equally thorough breakdowns for production schedules.

For much of Lombard's short but eventful life, people within her circle had a way of dying in unexpected, even mysterious ways. Ince would be the first, dying of an alleged heart attack after a 1924 weekend party on Hearst's huge private

WES D. GEHRING

Chaplin and Georgia Hale in a scene from The Gold Rush *(1925).*

yacht. That was the official story, but another murder-related rumor has persisted through the years. This dark scenario has Hearst being convinced that Chaplin was having an affair with Hearst's mistress, actress Marion Davies, both of whom were also guests that fateful weekend. Ince, who bore a physical resemblance to Chaplin, was supposedly caught with Davies by Hearst, who then mistakenly shot him—assuming it was the comedian. The newspaper magnate, given his phenomenal wealth and power, was then able—so the rumor goes—to institute a cover-up. So what really happened? There will probably never be an adequate explanation for this still controversial incident.

Ironically, not long before the yacht incident occurred, Lombard and her mother had met privately with Chaplin. The catalyst for the meeting was Lombard's selection as the queen of her high school's May Day Carnival. The popular fifteen-year-old sophomore, already a Fairfax High track star, was soon doubly excited to discover there was a Chaplin talent representative at the carnival. The comedian was screen testing young actresses for the romantic lead in what would eventually be considered his greatest film, *The Gold Rush* (1925).

Chaplin was a great fan of teenage actresses, both for his art and for his amorous private life. This has traditionally been attributed to the lost love of his youth—a teenage beauty named Hetty Kelly, who died before he could reconnect with her.[16] Regardless of the cause, the comedian was in the habit of interviewing countless young actresses, with the most promising receiving a screen test. Given Chaplin's Lothario-like reputation in the film industry, Bessie's friends strongly encouraged her to accompany Carole to both the interview and screen test.

A bemused Lombard later remembered Chaplin to have been pleasantly professional but obviously disappointed that she was accompanied by her mother. When he explained that the inspiration for the film was the infamous Donner Party disaster in which a band of snowbound American pioneers resorted to cannibalism to survive, she expressed surprise that the film was to be a comedy. Chaplin's work, however, was often driven by black comedy, such as his later dark satire of Hitler, *The Great Dictator* (1940).

The interview went well enough for Lombard to receive a screen test, but she lost the part to Lita Grey, who had had a small but memorable role as a tempting angel in Chaplin's *The Kid* (1921). It is interesting to consider what might have occurred had Lombard received the part because the comedian's subsequent affair with the teenaged Grey resulted in their November 1924 marriage. Would romantic sparks have occurred between Lombard and Chaplin? Or would she have used her salty language to keep the comedian at bay?

Ironically, Grey later lost the part due to her pregnancy. Georgia Hale, the eventual *Gold Rush* leading lady was, like Lombard, a former teenage beauty queen. Much later Hale revealed that Chaplin had allowed her to see several of the competing screen tests, including Lombard's: "I said to him [Chaplin], 'But *they're* wonderful!' Because I thought I was terrible. In my test I just stood there looking mad and doing nothing. And they were all laughing and such. And he said, 'That's what I want. That's the quality.'"[17]

Despite failing to win the coveted role, Lombard had the satisfaction of having her stock in Hollywood skyrocket after being screen tested by the great Chaplin (his child bride tendencies were not yet seen by the public as a liability). Indeed, when his first teenaged wife (Mildred Harris) divorced

Chaplin in 1920, famed Indiana humorist Kin Hubbard had his cracker-barrel hero Abe Martin note, "Mr. an' Mrs. Charley Chaplin have split up. Charley is like a whole lot o' other fellers—he kin make ever' buddy laugh but his wife."[18] After a 1924 court ruling that Chaplin's second teenaged wife (Grey) should continue her education, Hubbard's friend and fellow humorist Will Rogers observed, "This girl don't need to go to school. Any girl smart enough to marry Charlie Chaplin should be lecturing at Vassar College on 'Taking advantage of your opportunities.'"[19]

Continuing school was also a question Carole and Bessie needed to address after shooting the screen test for Chaplin. While she had not become a stock player for the comedian, the Vitagraph Film Company expressed interest in signing her after seeing the same test. Though nothing came of this either, when Lombard started her junior year the fall of 1924 at Fairfax High she had reached an understanding with her mother. Once a real film break came along, she could quit school. Lombard was about to realize her childhood dream of becoming a working actress.

Lombard at age sixteen (1924).

2

The Accident and a Comedy Comeback

"Who cares about your respect? I'm too big to be respected."
CAROLE LOMBARD PLAYING THE STAR IN *TWENTIETH CENTURY* (1934)

ALTHOUGH CAROLE LOMBARD'S HOPE FOR A CONTRACT WITH the struggling Vitagraph company did not happen, the minor studio managed to affect her in one stereotypically Hollywood manner; it requested a name change. Executives were fine with the Peters family name, but the moniker of Jane struck them as too dull. In the brainstorming session that followed, the athletic Lombard's suggestion of Carol, after a popular tennis player (Carol Peterson), was accepted as a more romantic name. (Carole with an *e* came later.) Such minor tweaking was typical of the era. For example, Lombard's film friend and costar Gary Cooper had had another studio change his name from Frank Cooper, which studio heads believed sounded too much like a common farmer.

When Lombard started her junior year of high school, she was not discouraged by her stalled film career. Carole and Bessie were early examples of what later psychologists would call "reframing"—putting a positive spin on an event normally perceived as negative. Both mother and daughter believed it was only a matter of time before a studio signed Lombard. The struggling actress also encouraged her school friends to call her Carole. Never an ambitious student, anticipation of a movie career literally made it impossible for Lombard to study.

Bessie gave Carole a special send-off from high school— an October 1924 party to mark her sixteenth birthday, after which they would fully concentrate on the movies. (Mandatory school attendance stopped at age sixteen in California.) By party time, however, there was more to celebrate than a birthday as Lombard had signed a contract with the Fox studio.

There are various stories as to how this came about. The contemporary explanation had a Fox director seeing Carole at a dinner party and suggesting a screen test. This version even has the actress remembering Bessie suddenly expressing reservations about the opportunity—"I promptly accepted [the film contract], although mother didn't quite approve. She thought I should wait awhile, at least until I had finished school."[1] Although Bessie might have had last-minute reservations about her daughter leaving high school, it now seems that the contract was largely orchestrated through some wheeler-dealer, behind-the-scenes activity by Lombard's mother.

The catalyst for this activity had been yet another false start for Carole with another Hollywood power player, Mary Pickford. Unlike her screen test for Chaplin's *The Gold Rush*, which came with no guarantees, a Pickford associate had promised Lombard a part in the star's *Little Annie Rooney* (1925), an uneven melodrama about a ragamuffin girl avenging her father's murder. This supporting role fell through because Pickford found Carole too distractingly pretty, or, as a *Colliers* magazine author later comically phrased it, "in no case was there ever going to be any young lady playing opposite Miss Pickford who looked like anything but a cow."[2] Bessie decided to take her daughter's case to gossip columnist Louella Parsons.

Parsons was a highly influential gossip writer, especially in Hollywood's pre–World War II heyday. Syndicated in William Randolph Hearst's legion of newspapers, Parsons's views, scoops, and film industry-fed information was viewed as gospel by millions of screen fans. Capable of both great compassion as well as vindictiveness, she was a power to be reckoned with in the film industry. Bessie moved the columnist with her tale of Carole's near misses with Hollywood royalty. (No one was bigger than Chaplin and Pickford in the world of 1920s film.) Although Lombard's mother could be very persuasive, Parsons might also have been moved by the fact that she had a daughter Carole's age who was interested in movies, too. (Harriet Parsons became a screenwriter and producer.)

Several Lombard biographers have suggested that while Parsons helped Bessie and Carole get their feet in the door at Fox, it was Lombard's mesmerizing beauty that cemented the deal with the studio's head of production, Winfield Sheehan.[3] Whatever the reason, the studio signed the novice actress as a contract player for seventy-five dollars a week.[4] In spite of the small salary, Carole was pleased to join the picture business.

45

Fox also requested, as if exercising some ongoing studio rite of passage, that she change her name. The studio accepted the Vitagraph-sponsored Carole, but Peters had to go. Besides having two players under contract with that name, Fox also wished to avoid the sexual innuendo associated with the word Peters. After a brief huddle, mother and daughter came up with the name Lombard, drawn from their old family friends Harry and Etta Lombard. The name was also an indirect tribute to Carole's father, since Harry's loss of a leg forever reminded her of Frederic Peters's crippling injury. Lombard loved this sense of a totally new identity and for days practiced various ways of signing her name.

Fox frequently broke in new women contract players by casting them in the studio's lucrative low-budget westerns. This would also be the case with Lombard. In addition to appearing with Indiana's Buck Jones in *Gold and the Girl*, *Hearts and Spurs*, and *Durand of the Badlands*, Lombard also worked with western star Tom Mix in *Dick Turpin* (1925). Lombard's later expressed displeasure over the limitations of these parts reveals, however, why they were reserved for beginners—little was required of them. "All I had to do was simper prettily at the hero and scream with terror while he battled with the villain," Lombard noted. "Never once was I allowed to give my screen love's opponent a good, hearty kick—as I would have done in similar [real] circumstances!"[5]

In later years, however, Lombard viewed these westerns as a metaphor for how to handle life's difficulties. The actress's columnist friend Adela Rogers St. Johns put Carole's philosophy thus: "When you see trouble coming that's too big for you to handle, move fast and keep on moving and save all you can."[6] This "fold your tents and cut your losses" approach is the axiom of a survivor, which is as good a description as any of Lombard's slow climb to stardom.

The ruthlessly direct financier J. P. Morgan was fond of saying, "'There are two reasons why a man does anything. There's a good reason and there's the real reason.' The modern biographer's task is to find the real reasons."[7] When this analogy is applied to Lombard's real reason for being a teenage movie actress, the answer lies in her fascination with film fame. This was a girl who used to linger after school at the corner of Hollywood Boulevard and Vine Street hoping to see a star drive by in an expensive car. Her then solemn promise to herself was that some day her name would "appear in lights on cinema marquees and I'll drive down Hollywood Boulevard looking just as lovely as they do."[8]

While Lombard became disillusioned with her western apprenticeship, she enjoyed her other early movie basics, such as the periodic Fox photo shoots and costume fittings. Plus, the opportunity to share studio stories with her circle of school friends enhanced Carole's status. When they were not sharing information about their active teenage lives, they were practicing their dance steps, particularly the Charleston. Lombard frequently won Charleston competitions at the Ambassador Hotel's Cocoanut Grove nightclub.

These weekly Friday night dances "almost always ended as a private contest between Jane Peters (Carole) and Lucille Le Sueur (Joan Crawford)."[9]

During Lombard's short tenure at Fox, she viewed her best acting opportunity as a part in a minor contemporary drama called *Marriage in Transit* (1925). Lombard, however, proved not to be ready to play leading lady to the more experienced actor Edmund Lowe. Her idea of preparing for their big love scene was to get a pair of vampish fake eyelashes that could "make a scarlet woman out of a saint, and [thus] considered herself equipped to make love to Mr. Lowe in a manner calculated to burn him down to the ankles."[10] Comically, her preparation, or lack thereof, did not make any difference—Lowe stole every scene they shared. But maybe it was just as well. Lombard later confessed that her sexy eyelashes had failed her: "The damned things stuck. I played a whole scene blind; couldn't get my eyes open."[11]

Magazine accounts of Lombard's career published during her lifetime often posit a polite lie at this particular point in her story, suggesting that after a year Carole resigned from Fox because, as she indicated, she was tired of being cast in dead-end westerns.[12] The consequence of this decision, so the story goes, resulted in a yearlong hiatus. Although this movie sabbatical did take place, it was the result of something entirely out of her control—an automobile accident that left her face scarred, and Fox no longer interested in her services.

Ironically, this minor fender bender should not have produced any injuries. Lombard had been on a date with a well-heeled young man from her Cocoanut Grove circle of friends. The duo was stopped at a light on a hill when the automobile in front of them inexplicably started rolling back into their small sports car. The collision shattered the sports car's windshield. Lombard later told writer-director Garson Kanin, "So all of a sudden, wham! And I remember how I thought it was just beautiful, like a fireworks explosion . . . [of broken glass] and I passed out."[13] A jagged piece of glass opened a gash from Lombard's nose almost to her right eye.

Lombard's life was never in danger, but her budding film career seemed over. When Carole's mother met her at the Hollywood Emergency Hospital, a new phenomenon called plastic surgery was immediately suggested, with various accounts attributing the suggestion to everyone from Bessie to a young intern. For this new procedure to be successful, the stitches for Lombard's wound had to be done immediately and without any anesthetic. If her damaged cheek muscles were allowed to relax, her face might be permanently disfigured. Lombard biographer Larry Swindell compassionately observes, "At that moment concern for a career was not with Carol or her mother, but there were plenty of reasons for saving a seventeen-year-old girl's face."[14] With all due respect to Swindell and this unique mother and daughter, movies seem to have dictated life decisions in the Peters home ever since Allan Dwan's discovery of Lombard while she played baseball.

Regardless, no anesthetic was used for Lombard's fourteen stitches, and follow-up plastic surgery ultimately helped minimize the scar. Her friend St. Johns observed, "It wasn't a very bad scar, as scars go. But for a girl who had always been very pretty, particularly for a girl who wanted to be an actress, it was very serious."[15] In time the scar's redness faded, and Lombard learned to further diminish it through makeup and camera tricks. In later years Harry Stradling, her cinematographer on *They Knew What They Wanted* (1940) and *Mr. and Mrs. Smith* (1941), declared, "She knows as much about the tricks of the trade as I do! In close-up work I wanted to cover her scar simply by focussing [*sic*] the lights on her face so that it would seem to blend with her cheek. She told me a diffusing glass in my lens would do the same job better. And she was right!"[16]

These developments, however, were years away. Initially, Lombard was devastated, feeling that both her movie career and life as she knew it was over. After all, her ticket to the privileged Cocoanut Grove crowd was tied to both her beauty and her film connections. Take these away and she felt her chances for romance, marriage, and children were gone as well. Author David McCullough insightfully observed that, "Biography is the story of the evolution of an individual, and often you see that person change and grow—grow spiritually, grow physically . . . grow as a consequence of some terrific conflict or ordeal."[17] Lombard's ultimate reaction to her facial injury was one such evolution of an individual. A friend described it as "the beginning . . . of her [thinking] philosophy, her inner life.

WES D. GEHRING

Lombard is photographed from her good side in this scene from
Mr. and Mrs. Smith *(1941, with Robert Montgomery).*

For she began to laugh at herself—and she went on laughing
at herself as long as she lived."[18] This funny fatalism, to coin a
phrase, did not mean reckless abandon, which was how
Lombard believed she had been living. The new goals were to
live life to its fullest and to be sort of a populist minister of
merriment. That is, bring joy to as many friends, family, and
professional contacts as possible.

During the actress's lifetime, references to the accident
often focused upon her bravery, such as the *Silver Screen*
article titled "Star Courage."[19] But an added component of
Lombard's new perspective was an iron resolve. She later

observed, "I can truthfully say that luck hasn't anything to do with success. Determination and tenacity are the important things."[20] In fact, Lombard eventually savored the righteous battle as much as any victory: "If you wait for everything to be just right in your life, you'll never get any happiness. You have to fight for it . . . and the minute you start fighting anything, you've won. The end doesn't matter."[21]

Coupled with this new Lombard philosophy—whether it was funny fatalism or a fresh tenacity—was a higher profile personality. Prior to the accident, Lombard had been neither a wallflower nor a take-charge sort. That changed once she came out of the lingering depression that followed the surgery. To use language Lombard would have appreciated, she was hell-bent on taking charge of her life. Though still without any aspirations of being a great actress, she was determined to try movies again. And as feminist film critic Maria DiBattista said of Lombard's pivotal *My Man Godfrey* character, "[she] gives more than she receives."[22]

The downside for Lombard was that she was considered damaged goods in the film capital. The young woman who shortly before the accident had been considered by John Barrymore as a possible leading lady in his next movie was now limited to modest parts in a local amateur theatrical troupe. Lombard could have cursed her luck, but as she later observed of misfortune, "I found out . . . that the best thing I could do was to forget about luck. . . . And . . . remember it is only your own efforts to succeed that will bring you 'luck'!"[23]

Lombard maintained her ties to the film industry and attempted to get back to "normal," which included dating and dancing at the Cocoanut Grove. Coincidentally, a comeback offer came from a Cocoanut Grove acquaintance. "Mack Sennett, that old master of custard pie comedy, offered me a contract," Lombard said.[24] Known as the "King of Comedy," Sennett had set the tone for slapstick screen comedy, from discovering Charlie Chaplin to creating the Keystone Cops. By the latter half of the 1920s, however, his position as the premier producer of comic short subjects had been usurped by Hal Roach of Laurel and Hardy and Our Gang fame. Still, the Sennett name continued to carry comedy clout in Hollywood.

Sennett's offer to Lombard gave her a toehold again in the industry. But she hesitated, believing that doing slapstick short subjects was a comedown from her previous feature film work, even if it had primarily been in those dreaded quickie westerns. "[But] my wiser friends . . . pointed out the fact that many famous stars began their careers between volleys of pastry—Gloria Swanson, Harold Lloyd, Bebe Daniels . . . and many others," said Lombard. "They told me that I would get much of the training I lacked. So, finally convinced, I signed. And now [1936] I wouldn't trade that experience for anything."[25]

The Sennett slapstick legacy later became synonymous with Lombard's screwball comedies. None of the genre's other major leading ladies, from Irene Dunne to Jean Arthur, could match Lombard's skill at doing physical comedy, whether she was bouncing on beds in *My Man Godfrey* or boxing Fredric March in *Nothing Sacred* (1937).

Ironically, for an actress out of work because of a facial scar, Lombard's good looks were pivotal to her being hired by Sennett. A staple for his comedy productions were the "Sennett Bathing Beauties"—sexy window dressing for his films. Originally Sennett simply wanted to include pretty girls in press-release stills in order to insure better newspaper coverage for his studio. As the producer noted in his autobiography, when that idea proved a wild success, the next move was obvious: "Get those kids on the screen [I told our people]. Sure, I know they can't act, but they don't have to act. Put them in bathing suits and just have them around to be looked at while the comics are making funny."[26]

Since the Sennett Bathing Beauties were meant as an attractive backdrop, they were normally filmed in medium and/or long shot. At that distance, there was little concern about Lombard's scar being visible. Sennett described this preference for an attractive figure over a glamorous portrait with more inspired comic diplomacy. "The face was [only] used for two purposes," he observed, "to hang funny moustaches on, and to be smeared with custard pie, plaster, flour, mud, eggs or anything else the director could think of to have thrown."[27]

Of course, if a beautiful girl with an unplastered face wanted to advance at Sennett's studio, she needed to be able to play comedy, too, and Sennett and his masterful comedy assistant, Eddie Cline, were confident of their ability to be mirth mentors to anyone under contract. Thus, during 1927–28, Lombard appeared in a dozen two-reel slapstick comedies, which were frequently supervised by Cline. The stars of these pictures included such period favorites as Billy Bevan, Andy Clyde, Billy Gilbert, Mack Swain, and Daphne Pollard.

By Lombard's third Sennett short subject, *Run, Girl, Run* (15 January 1928), she was prominently featured as the nominal star. This two-reeler was important for three additional reasons. First, it was the most biographical of the dozen films she made for Sennett. Carole played a prep school track star with an active social life. Her introductory title card put it in a comically naughty perspective: "Norma Nurmi, star athlete—once ran a mile in almost nothing—and was nearly expelled for it." Second, *Run, Girl, Run* set the pattern for the most successful of Lombard's later Sennett films—a campus romance peppered with slapstick, *The Swim Princess* (28 February 1928), where Lombard is the school's swimming star. Third, by the time of *Run, Girl, Run*, Lombard had found among the Sennett troupe a special best friend for life, Madalynne Fields. When Carole joined Sennett, Fields was the studio's designated funny fat person. (Silent comedy's ultimate fat-skinny duo, Laurel and Hardy, had been teamed the year before.)

In *Run, Girl, Run* "Fieldsie," as Lombard soon nicknamed her, took monster pratfalls, such as her attempt to clear a high jump bar, and prompted overstated title cards reading "Don't fall so hard—we'll be getting complaints from China!" Sennett had encouraged the Lombard-Fields friendship, maybe thinking of his own homegrown Laurel and Hardy. But he need not have worried about abetting the relationship because Lombard and Fields found they had a natural rapport. More importantly, Fields quickly became Lombard's advocate, encouraging her in everything from what books to read to pushing her to higher achievement as an actress.

Fields was Lombard's first friend who might be called an intellectual. She represented the more challenging lifestyle Lombard embraced following her automobile accident. Fields also was fun to be with and constantly supportive. By the early 1930s she became Lombard's private secretary, financial adviser, and all-around troubleshooter.

Before leaving the Sennett period one should note Lombard's frequent on-screen teaming with comedienne Daphne Pollard. In addition to being very entertaining, their comedy shtick sometimes anticipated Lombard's later screwball comedies. For example, in *Run, Girl, Run*, their dorm room fight sequence (track coach Pollard is trying to enforce curfew) is a precursor to the bedroom battle royal Lombard later has with March in *Nothing Sacred*. In 1929 Lombard told a reporter, "There won't ever be another Sennett's for laughs. Daphne Pollard and I were just in hysterics the whole time . . . [and Daphne was] the best sport of the whole gang."[28]

THE MUSEUM OF MODERN ART/FILM STILLS ARCHIVE

*A relaxed moment with Gregory LaCava (seated)
on the set of* My Man Godfrey, *with William Powell and
Jean Dixon in the background.*

The casual improvisational Sennett style also served
Lombard well when she worked with similarly inclined screw-
ball comedy directors such as Howard Hawks (*Twentieth
Century*) and Gregory LaCava (*My Man Godfrey*). Plus, the

Sennett period endowed her with the practical comedy suggestion of "just be yourself," a lesson reiterated again later by both Hawks and LaCava. Moreover, Sennett insisted that his players get involved in various behind-the-camera activities, "so Carole learned how a camera operated, monkeyed around with sets and lights and was encouraged to bean a director who mangled a scene."[29] For the rest of her career, Lombard displayed a fascination with all aspects of filmmaking. Had she not died so young, Lombard might very well have become a director.

All in all, Lombard's signing with Sennett had been a positive experience, providing a comedy apprenticeship and proving to Hollywood that Lombard had a future in film despite her accident. In fact, this early version of The Hoosier Tornado had proven so successful that Hal Roach, Sennett's primary two-reeler competitor, felt compelled to grace his short subjects with a Lombard-like beauty, launching the career of platinum-blonde bombshell Jean Harlow. Unlike the comic versatility granted Lombard at the Sennett studio, Harlow was more often used simply as a comically sexy distraction. In her most notable Roach picture, the Laurel and Hardy short *Double Whoopee* (1928), Harlow's brief walk-through is made comically memorable simply because she loses the long train on a formal dress, revealing a delightful backside. (In later years Lombard and Harlow became friends, in part, because Lombard's future husband, Clark Gable, made several pictures with Harlow.)

Lombard's first Sennett film (*Smith's Pony*, 18 September 1927) opened the month before her nineteenth birthday and her last picture for the King of Comedy was *Matchmaking Mamas* (31 March 1929) when she was twenty. Sennett and company had shepherded her through a difficult period, which went beyond the trauma of the accident and a threatened film career. In 1938 Lombard recalled, "If ever I was unhappy, it was when I was in my teens. That's because you don't understand anything when you're that young. . . . For only the things you don't understand have the power to hurt you."[30] The Sennett period had greatly contributed to reducing the power of the unknown in Lombard's life. Fittingly, the actress credited her Sennett schooling as being "the turning point of her acting career."[31] But all things considered, including the pivotal addition of Fields as a friend and adviser, the Sennett legacy also seemed to represent a turning point in her life as well.

3

A Climb up the Film Ladder Coupled with a Hoosier Homecoming

In Lombard's star turn in the Mack Sennett short
Run, Girl, Run *(1928), she studies the three R's:*
"Romeos, Roadsters, and Roller Skates."

MACK SENNETT'S CASUAL FILMMAKING HABITS ALSO APPLIED TO his bookkeeping; contract players were free to catch occasional movie assignments elsewhere, as long as they did not impose on his production schedule. During 1928 Lombard starred in nine Sennett short subjects *and* made appearances in five features. The majority of the two-reelers opened in the first half of the year, establishing her successful return to the movies. The features followed in the latter portion of 1928.

It was not a coincidence that three of these early features were for Pathé, the same company that distributed Sennett's short subjects. Carole's contract with Sennett would eventually be transferred to Pathé, long a fan of Lombard's comeback work. Consistent with this interest, the actress was best showcased in the Pathé features of 1928. After a bit part in the studio's *Power* (her character was simply referred to as "Another Dame"), Lombard was prominently featured in both Pathé's *Show Folks* and *Ned McCobb's Daughter*.

The former picture had a title probably meant to elicit added business from viewers who would confuse it with the comedy classic *Show People* (1928), with Marion Davies. Title trickery was not unusual for Pathé. A similar scenario occurred with *Power*, which was released a few months after the opening of an identically named German production starring the international film star Emil Jannings. Ironically, *Variety's* review of the Pathé *Power* joked about the movie's inappropriate title.[1] Regardless, *Show Folks* was an early sound-film hybrid, with a musical score and roughly ten minutes of dialogue at the movie's close. It was a backstage comedy-drama that chronicled the life and times of a dance team (Eddie Quillan and Lina Basquette), with Lombard as the other woman. *Picture Play* magazine called her "a very pretty blonde . . . worth watching."[2] Lombard, however, would not have seconded this verdict. One historian noted that during a "projection room screening of the film, she sat there stunned, thinking her performance 'miserable,' and afterwards ran off in tears."[3]

Lombard's position notwithstanding, Pathé was pleased enough with her *Show Folks* performance to next cast her in *Ned McCobb's Daughter*, labeled by film historian Leonard Maltin as a Pathé "prestige picture."[4] Although Pathé was not a major studio, it was several notches above the poverty-row status of Rayart Pictures, which had produced Lombard's first 1928 feature, the forgettable *Divine Sinner*. In *Ned McCobb's Daughter*, Lombard had a small but entertaining part as a waitress being hustled by a bootlegger (George Callahan). A critic for *Film Spectator* observed, "Carole Lombard repeats the good impression she made on me in *Show Folks*."[5] And the *New York Times* called *Ned McCobb's Daughter* "a worthy pictorial translation" of Sidney Howard's play.[6]

In addition to Pathé being Sennett's distributor, Lombard's move there made her transition to features easier in another way—many players she encountered there had also broken in with Sennett. The male lead in *Show Folks*, Quillan, was a Sennett alum who later fondly remembered that even in 1928 Lombard was "full of fun and particularly well-liked by the crew working on 'Show Folks.'"[7] The secret of her popularity on the set can be found in an observation made by filmmaker and author Garson Kanin, who directed Carole in *They Knew What They Wanted* (1940): "She wanted to be around, to stay with the feel of things [even if she was *not* in the scene]. . . . On these days, she would hang around the set, watching; come along and look at the rushes; talk to various members of the cast. She was valuable."[8]

Lombard's initial foray into features—small parts in movies sometimes being shot simultaneously—did not always grant her the freedom of staying with a production through its completion, as was the case with her Kanin collaboration. But even in 1928 this absorption with filmmaking was paramount in her life. The former indifferent academic pupil had become a serious student of the movies. Indeed, in later years she periodically generated headlines by tackling nonacting film positions. For example, in 1938 she worked as a Selznick International press agent for a week and penned the *Hollywood Reporter* article, "Every Actor Should Take at Least One Week's Whirl at Publicity."[9]

In Lombard's later marriage to Clark Gable, one of their many differences was that while she lived and breathed movies, filmmaking was merely a lucrative job to him. But in fairness to Gable, who was seven years older, life had been more of a knockabout struggle for him. While a teenaged Lombard dabbled in movies, Gable worked in oil fields and toured with second-rate stage companies. Movies were all Lombard knew, or wanted to know, until relatively late in her life. Along related lines, in her career breakthrough film, *Twentieth Century*, John Barrymore's character states, "I could cut my throat." Lombard's movie response to this statement might also have been applied to the actress herself, "If you did, greasepaint would run out of it."

Biographer Doris Kearns Goodwin has written insightfully about a profiler's "shifting angles of vision"—the changing perspectives an author goes through as he or she researches and chronicles a given subject.[10] Of equal importance are the various "shifting angles of vision" that can be applied to the biographer's subject. Rare is a life without these variations. In Lombard's case, one has a series of escalating periods in which she elevates her dedication to movies. It was only later, paralleling the beginning of her relationship with Gable, that her "shifting angles of vision" became less film oriented. In the late 1920s, however, following her automobile accident and Sennett comeback, Lombard was in her first rededication to film.

Similar to comedian Jack Benny, Lombard's later friend and costar in *To Be or Not to Be* (1942), the actress was often self-deprecating about her films, particularly her early ones. She was fond of saying her feature movie career started "with 17 flops in a row." While Lombard's early filmography would never be confused with blockbusters, many were memorable, from the aforementioned *Ned McCobb's Daughter* to a small part in *Me, Gangster* (1928), on loan to Fox. Fittingly, the latter film was directed by Raoul Walsh, eventually famous for such gangster films as *The Roaring Twenties* (1939) and *White Heat* (1949). Described by *New York Times* critic Mordaunt Hall as an "absorbing chronicle that points a moral in a subdued and sane fashion," *Me, Gangster* showcased many stylish touches. For example, the subtitles were in a handwritten style suggesting they were the journal commentary of the protagonist.[11]

Lombard's appearance in the critically acclaimed *Big News* (1929) boasted another soon-to-be celebrated director, Gregory LaCava. But this situation was different for Lombard than Walsh's *Me, Gangster* for two reasons. First, by this time Carole had moved from minor supporting player to costar status. Critics took favorable note of this and gave her more review space than she previously had been used to. For example, the *New York Times* opined, "Lombard, as the female reporter, is a step above the ingénue film heroine and manages her part with sufficient restraint."[12] Second, LaCava later directed the actress in her only Oscar-nominated role, the zany Irene Bullock of *My Man Godfrey*. A 1937 profile Lombard authored on her old friend explains the Lombard-LaCava rapport while working on *Big News*: "Gregory wouldn't know an inhibition, himself, if it socked him in the eye, or dropped from Mars on his devoted head. . . . He is even a bigger, better and stubborner extrovert than I."[13] In addition to being kindred eccentric spirits, Lombard then tellingly revealed about LaCava, "He claims that I am his female counterpart."[14] Moreover, LaCava's casual, often collaborative style was not unlike what Lombard had known working for Sennett. It was an approach under which she usually did her best work, be it *Big News* or *My Man Godfrey*. Indeed, some kudos for *Big News* read very much like descriptions of *My Man Godfrey*. One reviewer raved, "The picture possesses a tempo accented by an engaging ribaldry that makes it good to look at and easy to listen to."[15]

There were two reasons Lombard was hard on her early feature films. First, besides her aforementioned modestly self-deprecating manner, the actress was what would now be called a "control freak." By the latter half of the 1930s she exercised an unprecedented amount of control over her film career. (A 1938 national publication on her power-broker style would even be affectionately titled, "She Gets Away with Murder."[16]) Lombard did not have as much creative

THE MUSEUM OF MODERN ART/FILM STILLS ARCHIVE

Some "engaging ribaldry" from My Man Godfrey—*Lombard
(seated), Eugene Pallette, and Alice Brady watch
as Mischa Auer literally goes ape.*

input on her pre-1934 movies, and this was frustrating for
her. As her columnist friend Adela Rogers St. Johns later
observed, "she had ideas and intense curiosity about everything on earth."[17] Indeed, Lombard's creative passions could
be so intense that another journalist friend, Adele Whitely
Fletcher, observed, "All Carole's conversations should be
underscored for emphasis, with some words and sentences
doubly underscored."[18]

A second Lombard picture complaint that continued well past her early features was when critics reduced her to the status of clotheshorse. As late as 1936 she complained, "Some day I'm going to catch the person who started all this glamour stuff about me. And when I do, I'll cuff him to death with his own typewriter!"[19] Although there is no record of Lombard ever achieving her revenge, a good bet for that unwanted honor would be a critic for *Variety*. Writing about Lombard's second feature role as an adult, the low-budget western *Hearts and Spurs* (1925), the reviewer said, "The heroine, Carole Lombard, a newcomer, is attractive looking, particularly in the fashionable eastern clothes she is permitted to wear, but as for expressiveness she might just as well have been labeled 'for decorative purposes only.'"[20]

Besides the clotheshorse liability, just being beautiful undercut Lombard's credibility with some critics. Interestingly enough, one such example occurred on yet another western, the Fox Studio box-office hit *The Arizona Kid* (1930), in which Lombard played opposite popular Warner Baxter as a happy-go-lucky Mexican bandit. This was the first of three Cisco Kid sequels for Baxter, whose original portrayal of the character, in *In Old Arizona* (1929), won him an Academy Award for Best Actor. Regardless, the *New York Times* noted, "Carol Lombard is a beautiful girl, but it is doubtful whether she is suited to the role of [the treacherous] Virginia."[21] Though displeased with being reduced to the status of a miscast beauty, Lombard enjoyed both playing a villain and showing off her horsemanship.[22] Plus, *The Arizona Kid* was an "A" production, as opposed to the silent quickie westerns with which she had begun her movie career—films that she believed had "made me look silly . . . all I did was pose around . . . the cactus."[23]

Obviously, Lombard had become more serious about her craft by 1930, especially given her comeback of the late 1920s. A rare look at this decidedly professional young actress can be seen in a hitherto untapped June 1930 interview from the *Fort Wayne News-Sentinel*. Conducted during her first return visit since leaving the city in 1914, the article seems to have been lost in time. Even the best of the standard Lombard sources only vaguely dates the visit at the end of 1930, *if* they mention her return at all.[24] While no biographer had cited an interview, it made sense to this author that there was some sort of "hometown girl makes good" article, especially because her film roles were becoming increasingly important. For example, she had been third billed in the aforementioned 1930 commercial hit *The Arizona Kid*, while her first 1930 release, *The Racketeer*, had her playing second lead—a heroine movingly caught in a romantic triangle. Indeed, *Film Daily's* January 1930 review observed, "Carole Lombard proves a real surprise, and does her best work to date. In fact, this is the first opportunity she has had to prove that she has the stuff to go over. With looks, and a good trouping sense, she also has the personality."[25]

Consequently, when no reference to a Lombard hometown visit appeared in any late 1930 Fort Wayne newspaper, a systematic search of earlier issues revealed that the actress's return occurred from 17–18 June 1930. The extensive interview that surfaced, "Carol [not yet Carole] Lombard Converses as Easily as She Acts," reveals a movie-wise young actress, not yet twenty-two years old, entertainingly conversant on a variety of topical film questions. First, she noted the importance of a performer establishing a consistent persona: "It's personality that counts on the screen. A beautiful girl that can not act and has no personality will not make a success in pictures."[26] Though based in fact, her insight is also unintentionally amusing, given that it seems to document her awareness of the aforementioned *Film Daily* review of her *Racketeer* performance, and how "She also has . . . personality."

Second, Lombard addressed with poignant directness the commodity component that is modern film stardom. "Most people don't think we're human," she said. "Everywhere we go they just stare and stare at us. I guess persons in all professions are thought of in the same way."[27] Third, Lombard was comfortable with the sound revolution that had so recently swept through Hollywood, implying that "talkies" better enabled the performer to create that all-important personality. Yet, she modestly counted herself "lucky because of my low-pitched voice, for the 'talkies' were just too bad for the actors and actresses with 'squeaky voices'"—a phenomenon that primitive early sound equipment only made worse.[28] Ironically, one of the films then playing Fort Wayne was *Redemption* (1930), which starred John

Gilbert.[29] Gilbert was arguably the most high-profile victim of the transition to sound.

Ultimately, however, what most impresses the modern reader is Lombard's maturity. There is neither a sense of condescension toward a small-town newspaper, nor a negative word on any of several period stars about which she is quizzed. What most brings this maturity into perspective is the contrast between Lombard's article and another Hollywood interview, which coincidently appeared in the same issue of the *Fort Wayne News-Sentinel*. The latter syndicated piece is with Clara Bow, the famous "It" girl of the movies. Bow, who successfully weathered the transition to sound, was involved in a sexual scandal that irreparably damaged her career. In the article in question, "Clara Bow Says Latest 'Boy Friend' Expensive," Bow matter-of-factly details her casual sexual mores by way of an attempt to avert a $150,000 alienation of affection suit. Her sadly naive defense: "I met the man on the coast and fell for him plenty hard . . . I guess. I knew he was married but he said his wife didn't understand him. And he had such nice manners."[30]

Seldom has a movie star been more in need of a spin doctor. It is easy to see how Bow's career soon self-destructed. In contrast, Lombard was always her own best media friend. The Fort Wayne interview is an early, if not first, example of Lombard's winning way with the press. During the 1930s, Lombard was one of the movie industry's high-visibility performers in print formats, with many profiles essentially turning into Lombard interviews. Indeed, besides the aforementioned pluses showcased in the actress's 1930 Fort Wayne session, she could simply be informatively amusing. For example, the hometown piece also featured Lombard sharing comic Hollywood nicknames, from actress Gloria Swanson's "Swansonia" to Lombard answering to "Lombardy Limited."[31]

Interestingly enough, given that Lombard had initially been discovered for the movies while playing baseball, the only real media distraction during her Fort Wayne visit came courtesy of a major leaguer. The city's most notable baseball player, future Hall of Famer Chuck Klein, was back in town for an exhibition game between his Philadelphia Phillies and the hometown Fort Wayne Chiefs.[32] Fittingly, 1928 had been a pivotal baseball year for both Klein and Lombard. Klein's slugging prowess for the Chiefs had resulted in his being promoted to the Phillies, and Lombard had starred in a Sennett short, *The Campus Vamp*, where her hitting and baserunning skills were highlighted in a two-color Technicolor diamond sequence. Lombard had wanted to attend the Klein exhibition game, but her Fort Wayne homecoming commitments kept her away.

During her visit home, the actress, accompanied by her mother Bessie Peters, stayed at the home of her aunt, Mrs. F. E. Hoffman. In honor of Lombard's homecoming, an epic reception—*the* social event of several seasons—was held the Wednesday afternoon and evening of 18 June 1930 at the tony Swinney Court home of Mrs. Hugh G. Keegan and her

*Lombard and her mother Bessie at approximately
the time of their 1930 visit to Fort Wayne.*

daughter, Margaret Ann Keegan. Amazingly, reported the
Fort Wayne Journal-Gazette, "Several hundred guests,
including many who had [claimed to have] known Miss
Lombard when she lived in this city, called during the afternoon and evening hours."[33]

The catalyst for Lombard's visit has often been attributed to the death of her maternal grandmother, Alice Cheney Knight. Indeed, during the actress's Fort Wayne interview she said, "The studio would not have permitted me to stop off this long but my grandmother Knight recently passed away, so they gave me a short leave of absence."[34] Be that as it may, this was *not* the whole story. Actually Knight died on 24 January, during her annual winter visit to California![35] Lombard biographer Larry Swindell suggests there was additional Indiana legal business related to the grandmother's will.[36] Though quite possible, what really made the Hoosier stop possible was the actress's filmmaking obligations in New York City.

Lombard recently had moved from Pathé to Paramount, and her current project (*Fast and Loose*, 1930) was dividing its shooting schedule between Hollywood and Paramount's Astoria Studio in New York. Thus, Lombard's homecoming, though undoubtedly heartfelt, had a lot to do with travel convenience (Fort Wayne's proximity to Chicago made it only a minor detour for the 1930s transcontinental train traveler). This being said, however, there were three personal pluses that came out of the visit. First, Lombard was able to reconnect with a father who had gone out of her life much too soon. In fact, one of the aforementioned Fort Wayne reception hostesses, Margaret Ann Keegan, was the daughter of a close friend of Frederic Peters. Second, at the thoughtful behest of Peters, arrangements were made for Bessie to obtain a quiet divorce. He wanted to give her the chance to remarry, if she so desired. (Neither of Lombard's parents subsequently remarried.) Third, in many ways the homecoming was Carole's special gift to her mother. Despite Bessie's departure from Fort Wayne in 1914, being a Hoosier was still very much a part of who she was—no doubt more than a daughter who was only six years old when they left. Regardless, the old adage that "you can't go home again" need not apply when one can return with a movie star in tow.

Carole's Indiana legacy was largely tied to the practical, egalitarian values by which Bessie had raised her. Thus, the ultimate period compliment for either Carole or her mother was a term then popular in midwestern states such as Indiana and Iowa—"common." That is, they were individuals born to affluence who still acted like everyday people, or, as the *Fort Wayne News-Sentinel* interviewer phrased it, Lombard "graciously conversed in the living room of her aunt's home just as any mortal would talk to any other mortal."[37] In addition, because Bessie continued to be both Carole's chief adviser and best friend, the return visit (which meant a great deal to her mother) became a daughter's thank you.

4

A Brief Union of Consequence

Lombard's No Man of Her Own *(1932) character
is comically down on small-town life:
"Sometimes I go out in the woods and scream—
just to keep from bursting."*

SHORTLY AFTER CAROLE LOMBARD'S NEW YORK CITY-BOUND
exit from Fort Wayne, the actress's first Paramount feature,
Safety in Numbers (1930), opened in her hometown. Calling
it a "snappy romance," the *Fort Wayne News-Sentinel's* cap-
sule review observed, "Carol Lombard (Jane Peters), former
Fort Wayne girl, is seen in support of Buddy Rogers as one of
the Follies girls."[1] While the print advertisement for the film
gushed "Screendom's five most gorgeous girls compete for
his love" and "New, gay, daring and delightfully diverting,"
the less-biased national critics were equally kind.[2] The *New
York Daily News* called the movie "Lots of fun!" and went on
to state that "Carol Lombard proves [to be] an ace comedienne."[3] *Variety* predicted "good box-office stuff," while the
Motion Picture Herald labeled it "entertainment plus."[4] The
picture traded heavily upon the youthful charm and singing
of sometime bandleader Rogers, who in 1937 married "America's Sweetheart," Mary Pickford.

Though *Safety in Numbers* was not directly addressed during Lombard's Fort Wayne interview, related topics were broached. For example, Rogers was the first Hollywood star the interviewer asked the actress's opinion about. Lombard responded, "Do I like Buddy Rogers? I should say I do. He's a very nice boy. I knew him long before I went into pictures five years ago."[5] Lombard knew Rogers from the Cocoanut Grove, where Rogers provided the musical entertainment. Fittingly, that Jazz-Age period was reflected in *Safety in Numbers*. Rogers's vogue as "America's Boyfriend" did not last long, but it would be enough to propel this picture to box-office success among the young. Still, the movie's director, Victor Schertzinger, later confessed he had probably given Lombard too many close-ups because of her great beauty.[6] Despite this admission from Schertzinger, Carole had told the Fort Wayne reporter, "I really prefer to play in all-star [productions, such as *Safety in Numbers*] instead of starring pictures. It's much nicer and the pictures are always better."[7]

Lombard left Fort Wayne for New York for further shooting on her next movie, *Fast and Loose* (1930), an adaptation of the hit Broadway play *The Best People*. The picture's main claim to fame now is that the screenplay was by celebrated writer-director Preston Sturges, and it was the film debut of stage actress Miriam Hopkins. For the Lombard aficionado, the movie is memorable as the screen outing in which Carol became Carole. Numerous explanations have been given for the spelling change, including the studio's story that it was an outgrowth of the starlet's interest in numerology. Lombard later, off the record, refuted the claim: "That's a lot of bunk. But since they're paying me so well, I don't care how they spell my name."[8] The truth, of course, was a great deal less fanciful—there was simply a spelling error made by Paramount's marketing department. Because the name cards had not yet been completed on the finished film, the actress could still be Carol without an *e* on cellulose. But the studio deemed a change to the poster as too expensive for a supporting player.

Lombard, ever the free spirit, is said to have blurted out, "What the hell, let's keep it with the *e*. I don't think I've ever seen it spelled that way, and I sort of like it."[9] Strangely enough, however, years later some pre-1930 Mack Sennett-Lombard film shorts surfaced with the Carole spelling. Was this just another random mistake? The whole story will probably never be known. In time, Lombard saw the additional letter as somehow fortuitous to her film career, like a good luck charm. In fact, she later, only half in jest, told writer-director Garson Kanin, "I think the 'e' made the whole fuckin' difference."[10]

Unfortunately, *Fast and Loose* failed to please the press or the public. *Motion Picture* magazine's review managed to summarize both the plot and its reception in succinct fashion: "A rich girl falls in love with a poor boy, and a rich boy falls in love with a poor girl [Lombard]—with complications. An uneven comedy."[11] Still, Lombard's New York production experience on *Fast and Loose* served her career well and allowed the new Paramount actress to network with everyone from director Ernst Lubitsch to studio president Adolph Zukor. One and all were impressed by the young Lombard. When Bessie Peters joined Carole in New York (Bessie had stayed on for a time in Fort Wayne), the duo was able to take in several Broadway plays. In fact, playwright and sometimes actress Rachel Crothers approached Lombard about appearing in a stage production. Although flattered, Lombard was neither in a position to accept such an offer (she was under contract to Paramount) nor willing to stop a film career that was just beginning to blossom. A Crothers-Lombard collaboration might have been something special, given that both women were feminists who excelled in comedy. (Crothers's 1933 play *When Ladies Meet* won the Mergrue Prize for comedy.) Needless to say, Lombard was a more confident and polished person by the conclusion of her extended New York visit.

At the start of Lombard's Paramount tenure (1930–37), both her personal and professional life was eased when she hired friend and former Sennett costar Madalynne Fields as a private secretary and all-around "girl Friday." Although Fields had grown tired of playing the rotund slapstick buffoon, she remained an apt pupil of the movies and proved to be a savvy assistant to have around, soon rivaling Bessie as the most important person in Lombard's life.

Lombard next appeared in *It Pays to Advertise* (1931), a vehicle that cast her as the secretary/love interest to busi-

An inventive publicity still from It Pays to Advertise *(1931, which showcases its two Hoosier stars—Lombard and Norman Foster).*

nessman Rodney Martin (Norman Foster). This was also an adaptation of a Broadway play—a frequent occurrence early in the sound era as Hollywood attempted to produce proven talking pictures. The adaptation was most notable to Lombard as yet another example of the film capital's Hoosier connection. Both of her *It Pays to Advertise* costars were Indiana born. Foster (born Nick Hoeffer) was from Richmond, and the third-billed Skeets Gallagher, who played an advertising expert, hailed from Terre Haute. Lombard and Foster were teamed again that year in *Up Pops the Devil*, and Lombard soon became a close friend of his actress wife, Claudette Colbert. (Coincidentally, both Lombard and Colbert were Paramount players who came into their own as screwball comedy actresses in the mid-1930s.)

Film historian and Lombard biographer Leonard Maltin makes the crucial point that Paramount at this time "was committed to a slate of sixty-odd feature-film releases per year—more than one new film available to theatres every week!"[12] This staggering depression-era total, which was matched by several other Hollywood studios, was necessary to placate an equally staggering 1930s mass audience—three times the size of today's television- and video-distracted movie audience. Maltin's point was that for maximum studio efficiency, in this factory-like setting, there needed to be a certain interchangeable nature to the players. No less a period filmmaker than Oscar-winner William A. Wellman comically lectured 1930 academics, suddenly serious about film study, that it would be like "going to school to learn the aesthetic differences between a Pontiac and an Oldsmobile."[13] But the downside to an interchangeable player formula meant that a potentially distinctive performer, such as a Lombard, sometimes languished in less than appropriate productions. This was demonstrated in a *Variety* review of *It Pays to Advertise*, with the critic noting, "Carol [*sic*] Lombard managed to put the maximum of feminine grace and charm into a pale and rather insipid part."[14]

Lombard was better served in her next two pictures,

Man of the World and *Ladies' Man* (both 1931). But in these particular outings, she could be forgiven for not really noticing. The actress had fallen in love with the gifted William Powell, the name-above-the-title star of both these movies. Powell was fast emerging as Paramount's top male lead, though he was nowhere near the superstar status he attained at Metro-Goldwyn-Mayer later in the decade. A Broadway player during the 1910s, the thirty-eight-year-old actor primarily played villains during a silent film career that started in 1922. His transition to sound and good-guy roles was launched with a string of mysteries in which he played the S. S. Van Dine sleuth Philo Vance.

Though their first two pictures together were both released early in 1931, Lombard and Powell were already an item. Indeed, he gave her a Cadillac as a Christmas present that year. They were, however, the proverbial odd couple. In addition to their sixteen-year difference in age, Powell was a man of the world, and Lombard was, well, twenty-two-years old. As her biographer Robert D. Matzen comically observed, Powell traveled "in elite, intellectual circles while Carole bummed around much of the time, giggling with Fieldsie, salting every sentence with a 'shit' or a 'fuck.'"[15]

Still, the beautiful, shoot-from-the-hip Lombard was like no other woman Powell had ever known. On their first dinner date "they talked for seven hours!"[16] Soon the couple was dining together every night and calling one another three times a day. The actress, however, was sensible enough to see some potential problems. "Bill wants to travel . . . [but] I have to concentrate on my career," said Lombard. "When I can't go . . . he can't seem to understand—now. And if we're married—."[17] As the romance escalated, Powell became more demanding, wanting Lombard to abandon her career. The actress immediately saw red, telling him "she had struggled for six years—a long, arduous, grinding struggle typical of all who seek success—and she was not going to let that struggle go for naught."[18]

Bessie had made her daughter a feminist years before that term entered the popular vocabulary, and holding on to that career meant more than just being a movie star. The actress was obsessed with all facets of film; to give it up was unthinkable. She anticipated the movie-driven characters of director Francois Truffant's celebrated *Day for Night* (1973) and the cinema addicts of novelist Michael Chabon's *Wonder Boys* (1995), "who climbed into a movie as into a time machine or a bottle of whiskey and set the dial for 'never come back.'"[19] Not surprisingly, Lombard was quoted during her courtship with Powell on the "dangerous" nature of marriage, which "spoils beautiful friendships that might have lasted for years. The idea of two people trying to possess each other is wrong. It must be a friendship . . . a calm companionship."[20] It must also be noted that despite Lombard's youth, she had already been romantically involved with a number of Hollywood power players, ranging from Howard Hughes to Joseph P. Kennedy.

Despite her misgivings, five factors softened Lombard's

position on marriage. First, Powell stopped making unreasonable demands and started to respect Lombard's desire for a film career. Second, she convinced herself that the greatest love, or as the actress named it, the "Counter-Balancing Love," is "the love of two people who are diametrically different."[21] Thus, the Lombard-Powell contrasts created an opportunity for give-and-take, what she later likened to a "perfect see-saw love."[22] Third, not to state the obvious, but Powell was a handsome, sophisticated suitor. Lombard had had a crush on his equally winning screen persona long before they met. In fact, one of her pet nicknames for Powell was Philo, after his aforementioned movie detective.

Fourth, though Powell was closer in age to Bessie than Carole, the actress's mother encouraged the relationship. According to Powell biographer Charles Francisco, Bessie found Powell a "charming suitor" for her daughter because of his sophisticated air and "impeccable manners," possibly reminding her of her own socially prominent family background.[23] Also, both of the actress's brothers approved of Powell. This family block of support for the prospective groom was no small achievement, especially given Bessie's continued influence on her daughter. Plus, the numerologist mother was also quick to point out that all the "signs" were favorable for a 1931 wedding. Ironically, given Powell's initial desire to have Lombard quit making movies, a fifth factor helping their relationship was the actor's ongoing coaching of her career. For example, after the couple had attended one

of her film previews (probably *Fast and Loose*) a disappointed Lombard came out crying, to which he responded: "Dear,
you didn't want to do that picture . . . you hated everything
about it. That hatred shows in your work. You didn't mold
yourself to circumstances and you suffered on the screen
because of it. Now, when you don't like conditions you must
learn to make the best of them. You mustn't let your inside
affect your outside so the camera can catch it."[24]

Powell further assisted Lombard's career by hooking her
up with his agent, the legendary Myron Selznick, brother of
celebrated producer David O. Selznick, later famous for
Gone with the Wind (1939). Myron had a vendetta against
the Hollywood film industry based upon the belief that his
pioneering movie mogul father, Lewis J. Selznick, had been
unfairly forced out of the picture business. This payback for
his father boded well for Myron's clients because he orchestrated contracts with exorbitant salaries. He eventually made
Lombard one of the highest-paid performers in the film capital. (Her nearly half a million dollar income for 1937 was
thought by many to be number one among film actresses.)

Despite these pluses for the Lombard-Powell marriage,
there was also some negative Hollywood opinion about such
a union. Powell was part of a cultural clique that included
silent-screen stars Richard Barthelmess and Ronald Colman.
Like an upper-class version of Frank Sinatra's later Rat Pack,
being part of this Powell pack was the height of movie-capi-
tal cool. Not surprisingly, some filmland insiders believed the

Lombard and William Powell on their wedding day (26 June 1931).

younger Lombard was merely trying to climb the Hollywood social ladder. Of course, with Bessie's child-rearing philosophy based on honesty and directness, her daughter was never concerned with Hollywood gossip.

Consequently, the intimate and largely family wedding of Lombard and Powell took place on 26 June 1931 at the Beverly Hills home the actress shared with her mother. Only thirteen people witnessed the ceremony, with the actor's father, Horatio Powell, acting as best man, and the actress's brother, Frederic Peters, giving the bride away. Both mothers, Nettie Powell and Bessie, as well as Carole's other brother,

Stuart, were also in proud attendance. The only nonfamily guests were "Dick Barthelmess, Clive Brook, and Ernest Torrence, and their wives. Ronald Colman, Bill's most adamant bachelor pal, was noticeable by his absence."[25] The nuptials were followed by an elegant reception on the premises, complete with Powell's best champagnes and liquors, despite the wedding occurring during Prohibition. During the party one uninvited couple appeared, gossip columnist Louella Parsons and her husband, Dr. Watson Martin. Needless to say, they were made to feel most welcome. Sometime during the reception the bride and groom slipped away to spend their first married night at Powell's mansion on Havenhurst Drive. Though it might have seemed like a short courtship, the marriage probably would have occurred even earlier had Powell not had to disengage himself from a previous union. Long estranged from his first wife, Eileen Wilson, also an actress, he had not entertained thoughts of remarriage until he met Lombard.

Sadly, the subsequent Lombard-Powell honeymoon to Hawaii proved less than ideal, with the actress victimized by a series of physical ailments that included seasickness and a modest case of malaria. Even after the couple's California return, poor health minimized Lombard's film activity. Despite her long history of seemingly healthy good looks, Lombard, noted biographer Larry Swindell, had a chronic low resistance to such things as the common cold and the flu.[26] Moreover, she had extremely painful menstrual cramps. The catalyst for a patently Lombard comic take on the subject occurred when a Paramount executive questioned the actress's frequent sick days. "God switched the formula on me; there are just three days a month I *don't* bleed," she said.[27]

Though Powell embraced key philosophical differences (such as a working wife) to make the marriage happen, Lombard felt that the union constituted a major makeover for her as well. In describing her first marriage to Kanin, Lombard stated: "That's when I learned how to put a house together. . . . And how to take care of his clothes . . . I was the best fuckin' wife you ever saw . . . a ladylike wife. Because that's how Philo [Powell] wanted it."[28] In addition, just as Lombard later embraced the fishing and hunting habits of second husband, Clark Gable, she polished her literary skills for Powell. Although Lombard was a high-school dropout, this was not the stretch one might imagine. The actress had long had inclinations along these lines, from following the book-reading suggestions of Fields while they were still at Sennett, to Lombard's brief platonic relationship with former publisher and stage producer Horace Liveright. (He had hoped for romance but had to settle for friendship.)

Regardless, the Lombard-Powell romance seemed initially to assist her career, a connection noted by period critics. When she costarred with Gary Cooper in the sometime western *I Take This Woman* (1931, whose opening nearly coincided with the Lombard-Powell wedding), *New York Daily News* reviewer Kate Cameron observed, "Lombard . . . grows more beautiful with every picture. Perhaps it is love that makes her so enchanting these days; as you know, she is engaged to marry William Powell and the marriage is to take place any day now."[29]

Whatever fueled the actress's performance in *I Take This Woman* merits special attention as the first movie in which an army of important publications praised Lombard—a fact somehow missed by earlier biographers. The entertainment Bible, *Variety*, opened its critique with the prediction: "A few more performances like this from Carole Lombard and Paramount will have a new star on its list. . . . She has a face that photographs from all angles and in her playing never falters. Miss Lombard ought to advance rapidly from this point."[30] Even more significantly, New York newspapers fell all over themselves in showering Lombard with praise. In 1930s Hollywood, no critical establishment was more important than those from the proverbial Gotham City. One has only to peruse the period clipping files at the Margaret Herrick Library of the Academy of Motion Picture Arts and Sciences in Beverly Hills, California, to realize that only New York reviews seemed suitable for saving. The *New York Evening Post* said that *I Take This Woman* "justifies this department's long growing suspicion that Carole Lombard is not only the most exquisite looking of the Hollywood beauties but that she is, besides, an actress of ability, intelligence and poise . . . [who will soon] top them all."[31] The *New York Sun* described her as the "increasingly clever blonde eyeful," while the *New York Herald Tribune* observed, "With each new role assigned to her, Miss Lombard gives further indications that one day she will rank with the best screen actresses."[32] For a genre Lombard had never been overly fond of, this romantic tale of an eastern society girl and a shy cowboy had served her well.

Unfortunately, her next two screen outings, *No One Man* (1932, as a spoiled socialite) and *Sinners in the Sun* (1932, as a model), were critically panned. The always insightful movie historian and Lombard profiler Maltin later went so far as to label each picture a "turkey."[33] Ironically, the title *No One Man* might also serve as an explanation as to why Lombard's marriage was then already on the rocks. In a late 1931 magazine article about her wedding she was both remarkably candid and surprisingly unromantic for a bride. "Bill and I do, and intend to do, what we feel like doing, where and with whom," Lombard said. "But—we both know what the other feels like doing, and why. That's all there is to it."[34] Moreover, one might also affix an irony label to this article, since it is supposed to chronicle the actress's marital happiness! Strangely enough, Powell addressed his own reservations about marriage the following year in yet another article about their purported contented union. "Marriage . . . is dangerous . . . it professes to be able to control love," he observed. "It says, 'Now that you've said these words, you've got to go on loving this man or this woman.' You chafe under it, naturally."[35]

Not surprisingly, the couple had divorced by August

WES D. GEHRING

A domestic moment between Lombard and Powell
in My Man Godfrey.

1933. Although period rumors had her romantically linked to
various Hollywood players (including actors Gary Cooper
and George Raft, and writer Robert Riskin), Lombard's
explanation for parting from Powell reflected her earlier
reservations about their relationship—the age difference and
the threat to her career. "To travel now with Bill [his special
passion] would mean that I must retire from the screen," said
Lombard.[36] But more to the point there were "conflicting"
production schedules. "Bill would finish a picture and have
three months' holiday," she noted. "I would have to make

three or four pictures in succession, so that I couldn't play with him when he was free."[37] (In 1932 and 1933 Lombard appeared in eight feature films!)

In 1933 it was an entertainment cliché to say that a divorcing couple "were still friends," but it proved to be true for Lombard and Powell. They continued to talk on a regular basis, as well as look out for each other's careers, including Powell having Lombard cast in the career-making *My Man Godfrey*. The civilized nature of the couple's parting is perhaps best summarized by Lombard's famous comment, "I must like the man, or I wouldn't have married him in the first place."[38] Interestingly enough, a serialized period biography of Carole, upon which the actress was closely consulted, credited both the marriage and the divorce with helping her career. The former seemed to "soften her [screen] personality," while the "personal suffering" of the latter made "her an even better actress."[39] Regardless as to the veracity of this statement, what is important is Lombard's need to put a positive spin on the Powell chapter to her life.

In their subsequent marriages, however, both Lombard and Powell backpedaled from positions taken during their union. Powell's 1940 marriage to yet another much younger actress, Diana "Mousie" Lewis, endured until the actor's 1984 death at age ninety-two. Lewis, however, essentially retired from the screen after her wedding to Powell. Lombard's happy, monogamous union with Gable was seemingly only marred by the actor's occasional roving eye—a tendency she previously had embraced in her open marriage to Powell.

Before closing the proverbial book on the Lombard-Powell relationship, four significant postmarriage events merit noting. The first might be labeled a "rekindled romance," because shortly after their 1933 divorce they were once again an item. One columnist even reported that "friends of the couple say that a 'friendly' remarriage is imminent."[40] Their second memorable news connection was costarring in *My Man Godfrey*, which both Hollywood and America found ever so Noel Cowardish—their ability to work as a romantic couple despite having been divorced. The third event was the tragic 1937 death of actress Jean Harlow, Powell's fiancée and a Lombard friend. Carole helped Powell weather the loss. The fourth significant Lombard-Powell postmarital link seems now to have been forgotten by history. The triggering event involved Lombard's pivotal performance in Hoosier-born director Howard Hawks's *Twentieth Century* (1934), a movie in which both her costar (John Barrymore) and director coached her on the importance of being herself. But while the Hawks-Barrymore influence is well-documented, and will be addressed in the following chapter, it is Powell's indirect contribution to Lombard's act-natural performance that had been lost. Period articles, however, drew a straight line between Powell playing himself for the first time in the critical and commercial hit *The Thin Man* (another mid-1934 release), and Lombard's similar hair-letting-down performance in *Twentieth Century*.[41]

A rare romantically subdued moment in Twentieth Century
(1934, with Lombard and John Barrymore).

All things considered, Powell's ongoing effect upon
Lombard was probably immeasurable. And while she had
not cast as large a shadow on his career, he forever cherished
the sense of spontaneity that Lombard had awakened in him.
Powell mourned her passing almost as much as Gable.

5

Tragedy among the Many Loves of Lombard

*"You'd be lovely to have around, just to sprinkle
the flowers with your personality."*
LOMBARD'S SARCASTIC RESPONSE TO THE SEXUALLY OVERCONFIDENT
CLARK GABLE IN *NO MAN OF HER OWN* (1932).

OF CAROLE LOMBARD'S EIGHT FILM APPEARANCES DURING
1932 and 1933, she was at her best in *No Man of Her Own*
(1932), which starred her future husband Clark Gable. The
movie casts Gable as a con artist-gambler, with Lombard
playing a small-town librarian. While their film marriage is
based upon a flip of a coin, love eventually makes Gable go
straight. The critical establishment, especially in New York,
was ecstatic over the picture. But unlike the case with *I Take
This Woman*, where praise keyed upon the future promise of
Lombard's career, *No Man of Her Own* was clearly stamped
a critical hit in the here and now.

The *New York American* review was so enthusiastic that
an element of comedy entered into its praise: "'No Man of
Her Own' is a triumph for Miss Lombard, Mr. Gable and
Director [Wesley] Ruggles. The film mixes that beloved
brand of hotcha-cha romance with a lot of laughs."[1] The
newspaper also noted that "Lombard tops any of her recent

contributions and the old ones, too."[2] The *New York Herald Tribune* promised, "you will be surprised by the punch 'No Man of Her Own' really has, and by its reality in both acting and direction."[3] Even the often staid *New York Times* credited the "amusing" Lombard and Gable with keeping the movie "hustling along at a lively clip and sustain[ing] a pleasing illusion of handsome romantics and dashing humor."[4] Running its review much later than the newspapers, *Photoplay* magazine summarized the critical hosannas by being especially expansive with its praise. "Clark Gable devotees and fanciers of Carole Lombard should take to this one," the review said. "Gable in his best heart-fluttering way, and Carole, with lines as scintillating as her person and clothes, turn in delicious lovemaking episodes."[5] Even before the solid reviews, however, the movie had generated a comic buzz because of a gag gift Lombard gave Gable at the wrap party. The beautifully wrapped package turned out to be a large ham—with Gable's picture stuck on it! The gag received much publicity and was an early example of Lombard's future depiction as a "beautiful actress with a rollicking sense of humor."[6]

Ham or not, a great deal of the film's success was due to the star power generated by Gable, who was coming into his own as one of the screen's most celebrated personalities. The previous year he had starred opposite so many top female stars (including Greta Garbo, Joan Crawford, and Norma Shearer) that he inspired a national expression, usually given

WES D. GEHRING

Lombard and Gable in their only joint film outing—
No Man of Her Own *(1932).*

to an overly amorous male, "Who do you think you are, Clark
Gable?!" Thus, the *Variety* review of *No Man of Her Own*
even went so far as initially to claim, "Gable is close to the
whole picture himself." The review did add, "The good cast,
direction, and . . . comedy arising mostly out of wisecracks . . .
makes 'No Man of Her Own' acceptable film fare."[7] No small
part of the movie's success, however, was based upon flirting
with "*un*acceptable film fare." That is, there is a palpable sex-
iness to the Lombard-Gable scenes, such as their first
encounter when he gets Lombard's librarian character to go

up a ladder for a book simply so he can glance up her skirt. Or, there is the cabin scene where Lombard answers the phone in the skimpiest of lingerie, a segment "memorable enough to be used in Saul Turell's compilation film, *The Love Goddesses*, thirty years later."[8] The Lombard-Gable movie was made prior to the tougher censorship of the Production Code Administration, which was implemented in 1934. But one need not focus on the risqué to sing the picture's praises. This author was charmed by the entertainingly casual banter between the two leads, especially their early morning antics after getting married. (Lombard believes she has married a normal businessman, whereas Gable is a sleep-in con man who now must create a "cover" occupation.)

The movie is charmingly overloaded with witty dialogue that is liberally distributed among its primary players. For example, after meeting the romantically aggressive Gable, Lombard tells a friend, "The girl that lands him will have to say, 'No,' and put a knife in it!" Later, when Lombard discovers that Gable is a cardsharp, she still loyally observes, "You need a lot of rope; whether you hang yourself or bring the rope back, I'll be waiting for you." Near the film's conclusion, Gable's crooked sidekick (Grant Mitchell) poetically explains to her why Gable voluntarily took a prison term: "He wanted to get the mud off his shoes." And after Gable has done everything to make Lombard's small-town character feel at home in New York, she shouts from the shower, "Do I get the key to the city?" Gable yells back, "I'm phoning the mayor right now!" This produces the most realistically pleasing big laugh from Lombard, as if hearing his comic comeback for the first time.

With the screen rapport between Lombard and Gable in *No Man of Her Own*, one might have assumed their real-life romance would have dated from this time. Lombard later pondered the oddity of the situation with Garson Kanin. After calling *No Man of Her Own* a "pretty good picture" (high praise from the self-deprecating Lombard), she added: "And we worked together and did all kinds of hot love scenes and everything. And I never got any kind of a tremble out of him at all. You know, he was just the leading man. So what? A hunk of meat. Of course, it didn't help that I was on my ear about a different number [other than spouse William Powell] at the time."[9]

Presumably, Lombard had not realized that Gable was also on his "ear about a different number"—fellow MGM-player Joan Crawford. Indeed, MGM head Louis B. Mayer had actually loaned Gable to Paramount for *No Man of Her Own* hoping to break up their affair, since both Crawford and Gable were married, she to Douglas Fairbanks Jr. and he to Rhea Langham, respectively.[10] Crawford's explanation as to why she and Gable never married could have doubled for the reason Lombard pulled the plug on her union with Powell: "Much as I cared for Clark, the deep conviction that we could last was lacking within me and I knew it. I settled for friendship."[11]

No Man of Her Own was a holiday hit at the end of 1932 and arguably Lombard's finest film appearance to date. *Film Daily's* praise of the picture, which centered on the various genres embraced by the film (from drama and romance to comedy), might also have applied to the eclectic assortment of movie fare she surfaced in during 1933.[12] Lombard starred in the horror film *Supernatural*, where the spirit of an executed murderer enters her body and attempts to kill again. As a favor to uncredited director Mitchell Leisen, she accepted a small part in his antiwar picture, *The Eagle and the Hawk*. Lombard's other three outings for 1933 fell under a melodramatic umbrella. *From Hell to Heaven* was Paramount's answer to MGM's *Grand Hotel* (1932), where the provocative lives of various hotel guests are examined. *White Woman* finds Lombard in an unhappy marriage (to Charles Laughton) on a Malayan rubber plantation. In *Brief Moment*, the best of this melodramatic trilogy for 1933, Lombard plays a nightclub singer married to an irresponsible playboy (Gene Raymond). The plot conflict involves the playboy's reluctance to get a real job and not remain financially dependent upon his father. Calling the film's success a "tribute to the talents of Carole Lombard and Gene Raymond," the *New York Times* added, "The plot may be hackneyed, but Miss Lombard and Mr. Raymond treat it as though it were entirely new. An audience cannot help being lured into a favorable reaction."[13]

Lombard had been unhappy with her Paramount outings and arranged to be loaned to Columbia for *Brief Moment*.

Unlike much of Hollywood, Lombard had a good working relationship with Columbia's often difficult and dictatorial head, Harry Cohn. Lombard was on loan to Columbia in 1932 when, according to Hollywood legend, she responded to Cohn's advances with, "Look, Mr. Cohn, I've agreed to be in your shitty little picture, but fucking you is no part of the deal." Taking her strong brush-off in perfect stride, he adjusted his pants and said, "That don't mean you can't call me Harry."[14] Whether exactly true or not, it is consistent with the reputations of both individuals, and the record shows a good working rapport between them.

As a point of reference, however, on Lombard's "shitty little picture" statement, Columbia was not considered a major studio in 1932. While this reputation was changing by 1933, true credibility came at the 1935 Academy Awards when director Frank Capra's Columbia picture *It Happened One Night* (1934) swept the top five Oscars (Best Picture, Director, Screenplay, Actress, and Actor). Ironically, this pioneering example of the screwball comedy genre, which featured Gable, might also have starred Lombard. Cohn, Gable, and Robert Riskin, the screenwriter, lobbied for her to be cast in the part that ultimately won an Oscar for Claudette Colbert. The film's shooting schedule, however, conflicted with a Paramount assignment she was excited about—a dance picture with George Raft called *Bolero* (1934), directed by her friend Wesley Ruggles.

On paper Lombard made the right choice. *Bolero* was a

*Gable and Claudette Colbert in the classic that might have costarred Lombard—*It Happened One Night.

big Paramount picture, originally conceived for major star Miriam Hopkins. In contrast, Columbia still had the stigma of being a poverty-row studio. In fact, Mayer was punishing Gable (presumably over attitude, though the specifics have been lost to history) by loaning him to Columbia for *It Happened One Night*. Lombard was also fascinated by being part of a *Bolero* story loosely based upon one of her dancing heroes, Maurice Mouvet, a Cocoanut Grove headliner when Lombard was an impressionable teenager. Plus, *Bolero* allowed the actress to show off her dancing skills. Still, it is tempting to consider what might have been had Lombard joined Gable on the screwball classic *It Happened One Night*. After all, this was the genre soon to be synonymous with Lombard. Indeed, Columbia cast the actress in another pioneering screwball comedy, *Twentieth Century*, later in 1934. Consequently, one assumes that the actress would have excelled in the *It Happened One Night* part, especially given a Capra improvisational style reminiscent of Lombard's experience with Mack Sennett. On a personal level, casting Lombard with Gable might have been an early catalyst for romance. But such was not the case.

While reviewers considered *Brief Moment* as Lombard's finest 1933 cinematic outing, the thriller *Supernatural* has been helped by history, acquiring a cult following. The picture has also been mentioned as a possible influence upon Denzel Washington's chilling *Fallen* (1998), a film-noir tale of an executed murderer whose spirit "lives" on to kill again. Predictably, the more recent movie ends on a darker note, with Washington's detective unable to thwart an evil killing force that seems to be Lucifer himself. In contrast, Lombard's character does not kill anyone while under the influence of the murderous spirit. Thus, in the standard happy-ending tradition of depression-era America, Lombard returns to normal life and presumably a romance with leading man Randolph Scott. Though *Supernatural* was not fully appreciated until years later, Lombard's performance, as what the *New York Herald Tribune* critic called a "platinum Zombie," was not without period praise.[15] In addition to kudos from the *Tribune*, Mordaunt Hall of the *New York Times* observed that the movie worked "through camera wizardry to show the spirit of a dead murderer entering the body of a wholesome girl and causing her to behave like a savage. . . . Miss Lombard's portrayal [of this girl] . . . is praiseworthy."[16] Most contemporary publications failed to appreciate the thriller inventiveness of the *Supernatural* story, though the *New York Daily News* credited it with being "the spookiest of the recent pictures designed to expose the spiritualist racket."[17]

Coincidently, Lombard had a spooky real-life experience during the production of another 1933 film, *White Woman*. A chimpanzee being used for atmosphere in this jungle picture "suddenly flew into a rage and seized her arm in his powerful jaws."[18] Though Lombard's limb was badly lacerated, she insisted on returning to work immediately after being treated at the local hospital. This quick "get back in the saddle" reflex might have been triggered by the fact that Lombard's last visit to this hospital followed her near career-ending automobile accident, which had resulted in a long gash across her cheek. Lombard's brief reconciliation with Powell following their mid-August 1933 divorce came about, in part, by his concern over the chimpanzee-related accident.

Lombard's short fling with Powell was part of her very busy romantic life in the latter half of 1933. She was also seeing Riskin, a frequent Capra collaborator, who won the Oscar for the screenplay of *It Happened One Night*.

Sparks also flew between Lombard and young Russ Columbo, who coached her through two songs she had for *White Woman*. Columbo was famous for his rich baritone voice, very much like his friend and radio rival Bing Crosby. Comedian George Burns enjoyed kidding both singers, as well as himself, with the following comparison: "They both sang exactly alike and I couldn't understand it. Two guys, singing alike, and they're both stars! I sang entirely different and couldn't get any place."[19]

Lombard's appearance in *White Woman* had been followed by *Bolero*, where her teaming with Raft quickly provoked rumors of an off-camera romance. Although some Lombard profilers dated the duo's personal connection to the *Bolero* sequel, *Rumba* (1935), Raft biographer Lewis Yablonsky makes a strong case for their affair occurring during the earlier film. Raft kept a *Bolero* photograph of Lombard in his Beverly Hills home for the rest of his life and later confessed, "I truly loved Carole Lombard. She was the greatest girl that ever lived."[20] It may have been love for Raft, but it was more a sexy friendship for Lombard.

Ironically, in some ways Raft represented more of a match for her than the sophisticated Powell or the intellectual Riskin. What was more logical than Hollywood's resident tough-talking actress hooking up with an actor every bit as tough, both on screen and off? Indeed, Raft was not only synonymous with playing movie gangsters, he had ties with the real thing, including a close friendship with Bugsy Siegel, a friendship showcased in Warren Beatty's gangster biography *Bugsy* (1991, with Joe Montegna as Raft). In addition, Raft had started as a nightclub hoofer and shared Lombard's passion for dancing. Both Lombard and Raft also had very healthy sex drives. As befitted the actress's reputation for bawdy witticism, when asked by a reporter who was filmland's greatest lover, Lombard's famous off-the-record reply was, "George Raft [pause], or did you just mean on the screen?"

Remarkably, even this bona fide tough guy-lothario was unnerved by Lombard's relaxed sexuality. Raft later recalled the time he discovered the actress was not a natural blonde. Sitting and talking with Raft in her *Bolero* dressing room, Lombard started to undress in front of the actor. Soon stunningly nude, Carole remained, however, preoccupied with casual chatting while mixing peroxide and another liquid in a bowl. Though Raft expected a call to the set at any time, the actress continued to leisurely talk as she now began "to apply the liquid to dye the hair around her honeypot. She glanced up, saw my amazed look, and smiled, 'Relax, Georgie, I'm just making my collar and cuffs match.'"[21]

Lombard obviously had fun making *Bolero* with Raft, and as her biographer Leonard Maltin suggested, it had been a good career move for both performers, adding, "Her characterization of the hard-edged but vulnerable showgirl allows her to use her personality in a way most earlier parts had not, and her dance scenes with Raft are great fun."[22] Fittingly, Raft later chose to write about *Bolero* in his turn at the *Saturday*

WES D. GEHRING

A romantic soft focus moment from Bolero *(1934, with Lombard and George Raft).*

Evening Post's famous rotating celebrity column, "The Role I Liked Best. . ."[23] Lombard's leading man in private life, however, was slowly becoming singer Columbo. *Bolero* wrapped just prior to Christmas 1933, and by early 1934 Lombard and Columbo were an item, generating periodic Hollywood rumors of a pending engagement. During Lombard's storied romance with Gable, the actress made a now famous 1938 off-the-record comment to a *Life* reporter that Columbo was the love of her life. The surprised interviewer is said to have interjected, "you mean other than Clark Gable?" To this a decidedly serious Lombard repeated, "Russ Columbo was *the* great love of my life."

Much of the first half of 1934 was a personal and professional high for Lombard. In addition to having Columbo in her life, *Bolero* opened in February to favorable reviews, such as the one in the *Hollywood Reporter* that observed, "you exhibitors have a humdinger of an attraction coming your way."[24] *Bolero* was followed by the release of the box-office hit, *We're Not Dressing*, and the critically acclaimed *Twentieth Century*. The former was a zany but popular musical comedy about a shipwreck loosely based on Sir James M. Barrie's *The Admirable Crichton*. With an all-star cast headed by Bing Crosby, the movie also had elements of a new genre about to surface in American film—screwball comedy. Operating as a parody of romantic comedy and generously peppered with eccentric characters, the film's comedic quotient was largely filled by a supporting cast that included George Burns and Gracie Allen, Ethel Merman, Leon Errol, Ray Milland, and a bicycle-riding bear! But Crosby was the big draw, with the *Hollywood Reporter* suggesting all "Mr. Exhibitor" had to do to attract customers was "put out the Crosby banner."[25] Not surprisingly, 1934 marked the first of many appearances by the actor in Quigley Publication's annual list of the industry's top ten box-office stars.[26]

Although *We're Not Dressing* did not ask much more of Lombard than to be the beautiful leading lady for a box-office hit, *Twentieth Century* put her on the comedy map as a

WES D. GEHRING

Lombard and Bing Crosby finally get on the same romantic page in We're Not Dressing *(1934).*

major talent—a pioneering screwball heroine in a watershed example of this new genre. She more than held her own with the great John Barrymore, and, moreover, the mentoring of both Barrymore and the film's director, Howard Hawks, changed and elevated Lombard's career. The picture proved to be a critical triumph for all involved.

Columbo's professional life took off in 1934. He added

leading roles in movies to a successful performing résumé that already included nightclubs, radio, and recordings. The September premiere of his feature-film-starring debut, *Wake Up and Dream* (1934), had gone well, and almost anything seemed possible. In spite of their triumphs, both Columbo and Lombard shared an ominous sense of depression. Lombard later told reporter Sonia Lee, "Russ and I felt something cataclysmic hanging over us . . . [paradoxically], Russ was afraid that something was going to happen to me. I had been going from one picture to another, and I was frightfully tired."[27]

By late summer, with Lombard just finishing back-to-back films (*Now and Forever* and *Lady by Choice*) and scheduled to start another (*The Gay Bride*), the couple decided they might best recharge their batteries by some separate downtime with close friends over the Labor Day weekend. Lombard went with secretary-companion Madalynne Fields to a Lake Arrowhead resort; Columbo stayed in Hollywood with photographer friend Lansing Brown. While visiting Brown's bungalow home, Columbo examined Brown's antique gun collection, a hobby Columbo was considering. Unbeknownst to both men, an ancient charge remained in a French dueling pistol handled by Brown. The weapon discharged, with the bullet ricocheting off a mahogany dresser before entering Columbo's brain from just below his left eye. Though he lived to reach the hospital, Columbo died prior to surgery. Dr. George W. Patterson, a specialist in cranial surgery, was preparing to operate, "though he said he considered the effort to save the radio star hopeless."[28]

Columbo died before Lombard was able to reach the hospital. Through her tears, she managed to murmur to the press, "It is impossible for me to express how deeply shocked I am to learn of Russ' death. It is a terrible tragedy to me, as I know it will be to his millions of friends and admirers. The death came at a time when I know he was on the eve of his greatest success."[29] Additional period press accounts soon chronicled that "Lombard, accompanied by a nurse, [immediately] left her Beverly Hills home for a secluded cabin in the mountains. She was said to be suffering from hysteria, following the shock of Russ' death."[30] Not surprisingly, "Lombard went into a deep period of mourning," with Powell spending a great deal of time with her.[31] Although grief-stricken, the actor was impressed with his ex-wife's coping skills. She seemed much stronger than his new love interest, Jean Harlow.

Period front-page newspaper coverage following Columbo's passing routinely stated that the singer and Lombard were to have been married after he established his screen career. But in truth, their future together was a lot less certain than these press clippings, or a later Lombard *Movie Classic* article titled "We Would Have Married—."[32] Although there was no doubting the couple's love for one another, Lombard always had doubts about a *married* future with Columbo. He came from a large, close-knit Italian Catholic family. In addition to forever feeling the outsider, the actress also believed Columbo's traditional values eventually would jeopardize her career, as had initially been the case with Powell. Though they had been a couple less than a year at the time of his death, even this short period included several breakups, generally at the insistence of a questioning Lombard. During one such period Columbo saw a lot of actress Sally Blane (Loretta Young's older sister). Sadly, at the time of Columbo's death, Blane overplayed the part of the bereaved lover at the hospital. One filmland newspaper headline even read, "Sally Blane, Carole Lombard Mourn Young 'Troubadour.'"[33]

Columbo's funeral was an ordeal for Lombard—an ordeal played out on an epic scale. An audience of 3,500 crowded into Hollywood's Church of the Blessed Sacrament, with an additional crowd of 1,000 young female fans in the street outside. "Onlookers turned heads when Columbo's sister broke down as she entered the building and cried out repeatedly, 'He was just like a baby doll. Nobody knows how we loved him!'"[34]

Lombard arrived with Bessie, Stuart, and members of the Columbo family. Though steeled not to break down, Lombard cried throughout the service. Among the mourners attempting to comfort the actress was Columbo's friend and radio rival, Crosby, who also acted as a pallbearer. Crosby later paid tribute to Columbo by calling him "a handsome guy and he had a warm, ingratiating personality. He could sing, and he was a good musician. He played wonderful violin. . . . We were great pals."[35] Another demonstration of Columbo's popularity and respect in the entertainment community came from those who served as pallbearers with Crosby—comedian Zeppo Marx, director Walter Lang, and actor Gilbert Roland.

Carole survived Columbo's death by falling back on her fatalistic nature. "I believe that Russ' death was predestined," she said. "And I am glad that it came when he was so happy— so happy in our love and in his winning of stardom."[36] Additional factors aided in returning the actress to the land of the living, including her compassion for others and throwing herself even more intensely into her film career. Lombard reached out to the inconsolable Brown, who was "one of the most widely known photographers in Hollywood and numbered among his patrons many stage, screen and radio celebrities."[37] Lombard repeatedly told Brown that the shooting had been an accident and she did not blame him for Columbo's death. Though Lombard's words no doubt provided some comfort, Brown never fully got over the death of his friend. Lombard's fatalism was unable to rescue him from forever playing the accident over and over in his mind. Strangely enough, Brown's inability to recover from the tragedy further fueled Lombard's need to recover. She was determined not to be victimized by Columbo's death.

Lombard's second recovery component—an intensified career drive—will be addressed in later chapters. There are, however, two bizarre footnotes to Lombard's love and loss of

Columbo. The first, heavily reported at the time, involved Columbo's beloved mother, Mrs. Julio Columbo. She suffered a heart attack just two days before her son's fatal accident, and, consequently, his death was kept from her on doctor's orders for fear the shock would kill her. Paradoxically, she lived for several more years. But the elaborate ruse concocted immediately after her son's shooting death was never lifted. She allegedly died never knowing her "favorite son" had preceded her in death. The Columbo family and Lombard maintained this conspiracy of compassion by periodically having telegrams from "Russ" sent to Mrs. Columbo from around the globe— all allegedly related to her son's international singing career!

The second episode features a darkly comic twist that Lombard probably would have enjoyed. Years after the shooting, Brown's bungalow was bought by Rosemary Clooney, one of Crosby's most popular singing partners. Clooney was unaware of the tragic accident that occurred in the home's basement den until sometime later. The accidental shooting soon became part of the Clooney family folklore, with the children adopting Columbo's spirit. At the time Clooney observed, "Now my children, when they are a little afraid and it's all dark downstairs, say, 'Hello, Russ, are you around?'"[38]

6

The Starlet Becomes a Star . . . and the Queen of Hollywood Parties

"During the January shoot for Lombard's From Heaven to Hell
*(1933), Lombard, shivering in summer attire, turned to her warmly
dressed crew and shouted, 'All right, you warm, bloody bastard[s],
what's good for one is good for all! I'm not shooting till
I see every one of you down to your jockey shorts!'
Much to her delight, the crew complied."*[1]

BEFORE ADDRESSING THE RENEWAL OF ENERGY CAROLE
Lombard put into her film career after the September 1934
death of Russ Columbo, one must first briefly examine what
she had already achieved cinematically in this abbreviated year.
The jewel of her filmography was Howard Hawks's *Twentieth
Century*. Coupled with the critical acclaim generated by her
effective teaming with Clark Gable in *No Man of Her Own*, the
Hawks movie put her on an equal playing ground with
Hollywood's top actresses. At the time, the *Los Angeles Times*
was most articulate about both her performance as free-spirited actress Lily Garland, as well as its relationship to Lombard's
earlier screen persona: "Possibly the greatest surprise . . . is
Carole Lombard, who succeeds in showing an entirely new
and different side of her personality as well as her ability. Coolly
intelligent and calculatedly alluring in former pictures, in this
she vibrates with life and passion, abandon and diablerie . . .

[creating] the best performance that she has ever given."[2]

Predictably, the New York newspapers were also full of superlatives, but as longtime champions of her work, these reviews often suggested Lombard was actually recapturing a comic brilliance she had fleetingly showcased in the past. For example, the *New York American* critic's rave review of the "devastating, uproarious riot of mirthfulness" that was *Twentieth Century* went on to observe that Lombard's "creation screams in raucous harmony with the shrieking crescendo of the piece, she throws herself with perfect abandon into the maelstrom of madness. . . . Carole is herself again."[3]

However one might read Lombard's earlier films, Hawks claims to have cast her for *Twentieth Century* based upon the private person. The director saw Carole "at a party with a couple of drinks in her and she was hilarious and uninhibited and just what the part needed."[4] Hawks thought of her as a poor actress but a great personality—"marvellous gal, crazy as a bedbug. . . . If she could just be herself, she'd be great for the part."[5] Strangely enough, when Lombard initially had problems playing a spontaneous version of herself, Hawks found himself replicating a variation of John Barrymore's character in *Twentieth Century*, who turns an ex-lingerie clerk into a Broadway star. Hawks's goal was simply to find a personality free spirited enough to match the over-the-top acting power of Barrymore, America's favorite ham actor.

The teaming of the more established Barrymore with the less experienced Lombard was a pattern Hawks frequently

Lombard on the set of Twentieth Century *(1934, with
director Howard Hawks).*

used during his career, such as coupling veteran Humphrey
Bogart with newcomer Lauren Bacall in *To Have and Have
Not* (1944), and casting John Wayne with a young Angie
Dickinson in *Rio Bravo* (1959). The director later observed,
"I believe it's terribly interesting for the audience to see a new
girl playing with a man who's well established."[6] The process
needed a jump-start with Lombard, however. Intimidated by
Barrymore the first morning of rehearsals, the actress was

trying too hard. Hawks took her for a walk and said, "'What would you do if someone said such and such to you?' And she said, 'I'd kick him in the balls!' And I said, 'Well, he [Barrymore] said something like that to you—why don't you kick him?'"⁷ Although stunned by the freedom Hawks was sanctioning, Lombard finally grasped his nonacting directive and the subsequent shoot proved to be a comedy success.

As suggested earlier, this "be yourself" mission was not entirely new to Lombard. She had received similar advice from Mack Sennett. But like a great baseball player (a metaphor that actually applied to Lombard), there are times when one has to review the basics. That is what the tutelage of both Hawks and Barrymore meant to Lombard. Plus, the actress was probably better able to facilitate the "act natural" directive because her close friend and ex-husband William Powell was simultaneously getting the same "be yourself" direction while making *The Thin Man* (1934). Because Lombard and Powell talked shop weekly, they were able to embellish one another's performance. Lombard's journalist friend Adela Rogers St. Johns later suggested as much, noting that "being funny . . . [for Lombard] came to life under the tutelage of Powell and Barrymore and [Bing] Crosby."⁸ (Crosby had costarred with the actress in *We're Not Dressing*, just prior to *Twentieth Century*.)

During the making of *Twentieth Century*, Lombard and Barrymore became members of a mutual admiration society. Lombard later confessed, "He taught me more in the six

A comically heated moment between Lombard and Barrymore in Twentieth Century.

weeks I worked with him on that picture than I had learned in the whole six years I'd been in pictures."[9] Once again, much of this involved drawing upon the real person for the screen persona. Or, as a period profile of the actress observed, "She's the same way in real life [as in *Twentieth Century*]. It wasn't until the movies put the real Carole onto the screen that she became a sensation."[10]

After this breakout film for Columbia, Lombard returned

to Paramount for *Now and Forever* (1934), a Shirley Temple outing that also costarred matinee idol Gary Cooper. Though the film does not make use of Lombard's screwball talents, it was a good career move. Temple was just at the beginning of her amazing popularity, and as *Variety's* review of *Now and Forever* baldly but correctly predicted, "it has Shirley Temple and that virtually underwrites it for box office."[11]

Consequently, Lombard's pivotal commercial hit, *Twentieth Century*, was sandwiched between two other commercial successes, *We're Not Dressing* and *Now and Forever*. The latter picture was followed by another guaranteed box-office hit, Columbia's *Lady by Choice* (1934), the sequel to Frank Capra's acclaimed *Lady for a Day* (1933). Though not in a class with the original (Capra did not repeat as director), the sequel was a popular and well-received film. Lombard plays a fan dancer who adopts a resident of a retirement home as a Mother's Day publicity scam, but predictably clicks with May Robson's streetwise title character. Though essentially Robson's picture (she starred in the Capra original), everyone involved received critical kudos. The *New York Daily News* called Carole "lovely, lithe, and alluring," and *Variety* said she "does a lot for the picture . . . [being] forceful, vibrant, and once or twice she shows far greater power than in her previous work."[12] The *New York Times* best summed it up: "Ordinarily these copies [sequels] are sad affairs, lacking in the very qualities that made for the success of the original. It is a pleasant surprise, then, to be able to report that 'Lady By Choice' is an exception."[13] The actress's career was at a critical and commercial high, thus, part of her difficulty with accepting Columbo's death was squaring it with a life so otherwise perfect.

Just as *Twentieth Century* was a watershed professional experience for Lombard, Columbo's death was an equally significant personal turning point, causing her to throw herself into both work and play with an added intensity. Unfortunately, MGM's *The Gay Bride* (1934), the movie she was shooting at the time of Columbo's death, was almost universally panned by critics. Lombard may have been distracted by her loan status at the prestigious studio, home to Gable, Powell, and a galaxy of other stars. With comic scorn *Variety* even suggested *The Gay Bride* would consign the mobster genre "permanently to Davey Jones' locker down where grosses don't count."[14] For the first time in several movies, Lombard's notices were mixed at best. For example, while the *New York Times* credited her with "a comic gravity which is decidedly effective," the *New York Herald Tribune* blamed Carole as "being almost as bad as her picture."[15] Despite the actress's later fondness for calling this "gay bride" of the rackets her worst film, she was about to enter the most productive period of her career.

The comeback started with a sequel of sorts, a dance-picture reunion with *Bolero* costar George Raft. Titled *Rumba* (1935), the picture again cast Raft as an ambitious dancer, but this time Lombard's character is a wealthy patron instead of a fellow hoofer. A plot twist, however, manages to make them dance partners once more. Privately, there were romantic sparks again between Lombard and Raft. At the time of Lombard and Raft's last sexual liaison, Lombard's promiscuity was largely a product of both an absent father and a pioneering feminist nature—sowing her wild oats. After Columbo's death her romantic escapades were equally fueled by a need to blot out the pain of her loss. Between her 1933 divorce from Powell and the 1934 death of Columbo, Lombard believed that love had now passed her by. She would be damned, however, if life would play the same trick on her. One could use a period joke to further flesh out Lombard's position. The comic shtick defined depression as simply "anger without enthusiasm." Since Lombard forever oozed enthusiasm over a whole litany of projects and causes, it is unlikely that any form of depression would ever linger long with the actress.

Providentially, Lombard's reenergized approach to a free-spirited life soon complemented her developing image as filmland's favorite screwball, both on-screen and off. As Hawks's aforementioned description of the actress as being "crazy as a bedbug" suggests, within the movie industry she was already considered a screwball. From the mid-1930s on, however, America at large also came to associate that image with both Lombard's screen persona and the eccentric private person they read about in their favorite magazines. Indeed, as early as a 1935 *Photoplay* piece titled "How

Carole Lombard Plans a Party," writer Julie Lang Hunt documented that the actress had long "displayed a fine flare for creating parties based on an idea, usually an absurd idea at that, and carrying them to a sublime finish."[16] What the article entertainingly documents, however, is that Lombard's eccentricity is planned—not false but ever so thoroughly mapped out. Lombard was a thinking screwball. And now, as Lombard biographer Robert D. Matzen observed, the actress had "entered her party phase."[17]

After *Rumba*, Lombard hit a major movie home run with *Hands Across the Table* (1935). The project started out on shaky ground. It was to be the first film supervised by celebrated director Ernst Lubitsch, now in a new position as production manager for financially troubled Paramount. Paradoxically, while the film found critical praise as yet another example of the "Lubitsch touch" (an ambiance of sophisticated comic detail and offscreen suggestion), the film was actually a happy result of Lombard acting as an unofficial producer. Lubitsch had wanted to pull the plug on the film.

The alleged problem was that the director of *Hands Across the Table*, Mitchell Leisen, was inexperienced in comedy and its leading man, Fred MacMurray, was simply inexperienced. Leisen later credited Lombard for making the difference, almost, in fact, doubling as a codirector. "She had none of what you might call the 'star temperament,'" said Leisen. "She felt that all the others had to be good or it wouldn't matter how good she was. She got right in there

WES D. GEHRING

Lombard and Fred MacMurray in their first teaming—
Hands Across the Table *(1935).*

and pitched. One day I caught her sitting on top of Fred, pounding his chest with her fists and saying, 'Now Uncle Fred, you be funny or I'll pluck your eyebrows out!'"[18]

If possible, MacMurray was even more generous with praise for Lombard. "I owe so much of that performance and my subsequent career to her," he said. "She worked with me on every scene."[19] So effective was their screen chemistry that they were later teamed in three additional critical and commercial hits—*The Princess Comes Across* (1936), *Swing High, Swing Low,* and *True Confession* (both 1937, with Leisen directing the former film). Still, *Hands Across the Table* was the best of this group. (Surprisingly enough, the romantic comedy duo of Lombard and MacMurray was much more successful at the box office than the now highly celebrated 1930s teamings of Cary Grant and Katharine Hepburn.)

The critics fell all over themselves praising *Hands Across the Table*, often comparing it to Frank Capra's watershed romantic comedy, *It Happened One Night* (1934). The brilliant young *New York Times* reviewer Andre Sennwald stated, "Of all the numerous efforts to recapture the mood of 'It Happened One Night,' the new photoplay at the Paramount [theater] is easily the most successful." *New York Evening Journal* critic Rose Pelswick observed, "a diverting film done in the same vein as the now historic Colbert-Gable opus is the week's new fare."[20] The *New York Daily News* also chronicled how enthusiastically audiences were responding to the picture.[21] The *New York Sun* was pleased that Lombard was not "disguised" under the "heavy makeup" which had so often taken away from her natural beauty in earlier films.[22] (The actress seemingly took this review to heart, she quit wearing thick mascara after this movie.)

Consistent with that natural look, both Lombard and the movie were critically complimented for being believable, starting with the actress's cynical manicurist, hence the title, *Hands Across the Table*.[23] This naturalism separates the film from the sometimes mistaken label of screwball comedy, which is famous for its entertainingly exaggerated zany behavior, such as Lombard's off-the-wall performance in *Twentieth Century* (1934). In *Hands Across the Table* Lombard is a complex, scheming, depression-era survivor out for a rich husband. Her life only gets more complicated when she reluctantly falls in love with MacMurray's impoverished American aristocrat. That being said, however, one of the film's most refreshing traits is its ability to allow the believable heroine to occasionally fluctuate from bright, yet standard, romantic patter to a broader comic shtick normally associated with personality comedians such as the Marx Brothers. A case in point is the *Hands Across the Table* scene where Lombard pretends to be a less-than-bright long-distance telephone operator, complete with daffy voice. Interestingly enough, Groucho Marx also did an equally winning dimwitted long-distance telephone operator in *A Day at the Races* (1937), two years after *Hands Across the Table*. *Liberty Magazine*'s critic, Beverly Hills, put Lombard's performance in the most succinct perspective: "Miss Lombard has not given a better performance . . . since the fireworks of her role in 'Twentieth Century.'"[24]

The November 1935 opening of *Hands Across the Table* brought Lombard's year to a triumphant conclusion. Things would only get better, both professionally and privately, in 1936. Her hit movies for the year included the great *My Man Godfrey*, her only Oscar-nominated role. Plus, she would once more find love—this time in a relationship with Gable. Their 1939 marriage was arguably Hollywood's most celebrated union since that of Douglas Fairbanks Sr. and Mary Pickford in the 1920s. In order to begin the road to both Gable and *My Man Godfrey*, one should return to Lombard's status as filmdom's most giftedly eccentric party giver. The seeds of both her final marriage and her greatest film began through parties.

What constituted a Lombard event? First, it was usually an unprecedented entertainment idea, such as the night she rented the local Ocean Park Amusement Pier for her party. At her famous hospital blowout, Lombard met her guests at the door in a nurse's uniform and issued long hospital gowns to everyone. The guests were then escorted to white iron beds with names and charts on the footboards, and medicinal-looking cocktails were served in glass tubes by a butler dressed as an intern. Dinner arrived in bedpans on an operating table, with surgical instruments doubling as silverware. Other Lombard festivities embraced a range of themes, varying from a Roman banquet to a barnyard jamboree. Second, these parties often had a satirical twist. For example, the hospital bash was inspired by the propensity of her friends to complain about their health, while the Roman banquet was prompted by pals complaining they were too tired to sit up straight at a table.

Third, Lombard's gatherings were strictly egalitarian—guests of all economic levels, from studio carpenters to studio stars, rubbed shoulders. And heaven help anyone putting on airs. Lombard had many pet peeves, but few things riled her more than people without a democratic mentality. Indeed,

Mark Twain's (one of Lombard's favorite authors) comic take on anger could have been coined for the actress: "It takes me a long time to lose my temper but once lost I could not find it with a dog." Finally, no hostess tried harder to please her guests. But while this made her the ideal party giver, the need to please sometimes created a misleading mindset in her personal relationships. That is, the tendency for men to fall in love with her was often escalated by the frequency in which she remade herself in their mold, whether it was playing the literary intellectual for Powell or becoming the outdoor type for Gable. Fittingly, Carole's take on her acting style, as "a follower" (emulating the method of her film costar), was also consistent with this philosophy of compatibility.

Though Lombard was the period's uncontested champion party giver, she first caught Gable's attention at someone else's bash, a formal (white wear only) noon party given by producer David O. Selznick's millionaire business partner Jock Whitney. Though ever-so eccentric herself, Lombard later observed, "You know those society mucky-mucks. They think of all kinds of craziness."[25] It did not take the iconoclastic Lombard long to concoct an entrance that honored the white dress code and still generated a laugh. Maybe thinking of her earlier hospital party, the actress noted, "I got my doctor to get me what somebody in a hospital would wear. One of those white things that ties in the back, you know, with your ass out."[26] She accessorized the outfit with a white mask for her face, white bandages for her head, a white stretcher, and a white ambulance. Then, fashionably late, to guarantee a special entrance, she was delivered to the gala with sirens blaring. Two interns in white carried this vision in hospital white into the mansion.

Ironically, the guests first rushed to her "horror-stricken, thinking she had been injured—and found her laughing at them."[27] The gag especially appealed to Gable, who always felt uncomfortable at formal gatherings, or maybe it was that provocative hospital gown Lombard wore. She later told Garson Kanin, in her trademark earthy style, "And for some reason, this [arrival] got to ol' Clark. He thought it was hot stuff. Who knows? Maybe with all that white he thought I was a virgin or something."[28]

It appears, however, that Lombard was equally smitten. The week following the Whitney party, on Valentine's Day 1936, Lombard had a dilapidated Model-T Ford covered with painted hearts and delivered to Gable. The gag worked on several levels. First, thanks in no small part to the anti-heroic films of Laurel and Hardy and W. C. Fields, the Model-T was America's favorite joke of a car. Second, Lombard compounded the comedy by giving him the most battered example of this automobile. And third, a Model-T spoofed one of Gable's most passionate interests—collecting expensive and stylish automobiles. Charmed by the gift, Gable immediately drove to Lombard's home and insisted they go for a joyride. The wheezing Model-T somehow managed to deliver the couple to the Trocadero nightclub, and their romance was off and running.

Appropriately, the catalyst to the start of their relationship was perpetuated in the frequent gag gifts they gave each other. Lombard even had a photo of Gable on a rocking horse blown up to life size and delivered to him—with real horse manure arranged around the bottom. The darkly comic Lombard also occasionally gave Gable a dead cat, an idea probably drawn from Twain's *Tom Sawyer*. After one such deceased cat present, Gable went comically macabre on Lombard, giving her a stuffed nanny goat in return.

Lombard's party mentality not only was the catalyst for the start of her relationship with Gable, but it was also the key to her receiving the part of a lifetime—as zany heiress Irene Bullock in Universal's *My Man Godfrey* (1936). The studio wanted to obtain Powell from MGM for the title role, but the actor would only accept if his costar was Lombard. Powell believed Lombard would be perfect for the picture both because of the actress's ability to play the screwball *and* her association with party activity, as the film opens with an epic scavenger hunt for a "forgotten man." Ever the gentleman, however, Powell also demanded that his request for Lombard be kept secret. He did not want her to think some pity factor was at work. Appropriately enough, this quiet kindness also mirrored Lombard's own "I don't want any credit" philosophy when doing the proverbial good deed. (The actress was known as one of the easiest touches for aid in Hollywood history.)

Without realizing it at the time, Lombard repaid Powell's kindness early on in the movie's production. While he had arranged for Lombard's involvement in the picture, she knew *Godfrey* director Gregory LaCava. As the following chapter will document, the casually improvisational LaCava devised a party atmosphere while shooting the film. This seemingly less-than-professional approach initially concerned Powell. Lombard eased the actor's mind, however, by telling him to trust LaCava—the director's unorthodox approach got results. Plus, the actress reminded her ex-husband that *Godfrey* was a new variety (screwball) of comedy that seemed to elicit an improvisational, off-the-cuff style, such as when Lombard did *Twentieth Century* for Hawks. Powell's reservations were similar to concerns Grant expressed the following year on another screwball classic, director Leo McCarey's *The Awful Truth*. McCarey, the comedy artist who originally teamed and molded Laurel and Hardy, was the king of improvisation. Grant initially wanted out of *The Awful Truth*, believing McCarey did not have a clue about film-making, but he preserved and garnered the best reviews of his career. Thanks to Lombard, a similar fate awaited Powell on *Godfrey*, with the movie becoming one of the seminal works of the Great Depression.

7

Lombard's Memorable 1936

*"Her entry on a set often occasions so many greetings from
propmen, mechanics, assistant directors and electricians on
the rafters far above the set that the uproar sounds like
a reunion between Tarzan and his monkeys."[1]*

BEFORE EXAMINING CAROLE LOMBARD'S FILM OF FILMS, *MY
Man Godfrey*, it should be noted that 1936 also marked her
appearance in two other entertaining comedies—*Love
before Breakfast* (*The Taming of the Shrew*, screwball style)
and *The Princess Comes Across* (a screwball mixture of murder and mirth). Though neither are in a league with *Godfrey*,
they would constitute highlights on the filmography of any
actress. Of the two, *Princess* is the superior picture. Indeed,
the film deserves a revisionist elevation to near-great status,
not unlike Lombard's underrated outing with Clark Gable in
No Man of Her Own.

Screwball comedy usually showcases a domineering
eccentric woman in a romantically skewered story that
includes little respect for anyone or anything, as described by
the title of a Lombard classic of the genre, *Nothing Sacred*
(1937). Consequently, in addition to screwball's tendency to
derail the conventional love story, there is also a proclivity for

satire, ranging from comic attacks on high society (as in *Godfrey*), to the period's propensity to mock big-city journalism, especially in *Nothing Sacred*. In *Princess*, however, the satirical stakes are delightfully focused, with Lombard doing a film-length takeoff on Greta Garbo, MGM's high-art transplant from Sweden. The *Princess* premise has Lombard as a Brooklyn-born showgirl, Wanda Nash, who is trying to jumpstart a movie career. Finding herself in Europe, Wanda decides to reinvent herself as Olga, a Swedish princess interested in a film career. A studio buys into the scam and gives Olga a contract. The movie then chronicles her transatlantic ocean-liner trip back to the United States accompanied by a comic sidekick (Alison Skipworth). The murder subplot (no stranger to screwball comedy after the critical and commercial success of the comic whodunit *The Thin Man*) involves the death of a passenger who had been blackmailing Lombard's wanna-be film actress.

Both the movie and Lombard received uniformly excellent notices. *Variety* called her Garbo impersonation a "swell characterization and makes a highly diverting [comedy] contrast when the 'princess' lapses into her real self and unloads a line of Brooklynese."[2] The *New York American* described the picture as "delightful and exceptional film fare . . . filled with fun, humor and spiked with thrills."[3] Lombard, long the darling of most New York City movie reviewers, managed to make additional converts thanks to *Princess*. Howard Barnes of the *New York Herald Tribune* observed, "As one who has not been

impressed by Miss Lombard's histronics in the past, it is pleasant to report that she gives an assured and restrained portrayal
. . . [which] is resourceful in exploiting its comic possibilities."[4]
The *New York Post*'s Thornton Delehanty credited *Princess*
with being the "first role in which we have admired her since
the early days of her picture career."[5]

Lombard was personally taken with *Princess* because it
allowed her to do what she had first practiced in those bygone
childhood days back in Indiana—mimic a figure from the silver screen. The fact that her impersonation would now also
surface on the big screen still felt like a miracle to her. The
joy over the success of *Princess* was, however, just a warm-up
for *My Man Godfrey*. Not only did she turn in the greatest
performance of her career, but everyone else was also at the
top of their game. Whereas Lombard's satiric Garbo had
been the whole show in *Princess*, *Godfrey* costarred an
equally diverting William Powell, as well as a superior supporting cast.

A lion's share of credit for the unique achievement that is
Godfrey must go to Lombard's loopy friend Gregory LaCava,
who directed the picture. His casual improvisational style
scored its greatest triumph with *Godfrey*, garnering him an
Academy Award nomination for Best Director. LaCava later
described his eccentric formula for screwball comedy success
to his drinking companion, W. C. Fields, member of America's
pantheon of screen comedians. LaCava mixed shooting "whatever came to mind" with maintaining "a sort of [alcoholic] party

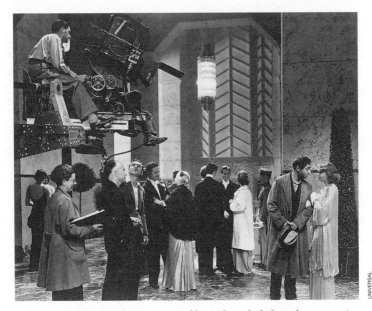

UNIVERSAL

LaCava on the set of My Man Godfrey *(directly below the camera),
with Lombard and William Powell on the far right.*

atmosphere on the set."[6] As W. C. Field's biographer Robert
Lewis Taylor observed, "the picture [*Godfrey*] was by no
means made possible by liquor, but LaCava believes that his
keen analysis of the causes and cures of scenario tension was
much appreciated by the company [cast and crew]."[7] That is,
the director used a party-time climate to encourage a collaborative mindset on his pictures. Pandro S. Berman, LaCava's
friend and sometimes producer, said, "Greg was most off-the-
cuff creative when he was drinking. And his career only stalled

when his doctors told him to go on the wagon in the 1940s."[8]

LaCava's approach was also documented by Lombard in a magazine article with the punning title, "My Man Gregory." Moreover, according to the actress, partying helped LaCava like everyone on a shoot and "he MUST like . . . the cast, the workers, the technicians, the cameramen, anyone or anything else that has anything to do with the making of that particular picture."[9] This creative party atmosphere was a circular phenomenon; LaCava dominated the improvisation. For example, Lombard remembered a *Godfrey* moment when the director wanted some quiet for his writing. As the set only seemed to get louder, LaCava observed, "'As long as we are NOT going to have QUIET, we may as well have a lot of it.' He rather liked that line so he used it in the dialogue for Irene [Lombard's character]."[10]

Following LaCava's monster hit, *Stage Door* (1937), the director was still using Lombard and Powell as examples of how his system worked. "Give me real people to work with, people like Bill Powell and Carole Lombard, and we'll give you a picture. . . . When I direct them I tell them to use their own personalities, not to assume someone else's," LaCava said.[11] Fittingly, this "be yourself" approach paralleled Howard Hawks's earlier direction for Lombard to act natural in *Twentieth Century*. All this is not to imply Lombard was as kooky as her *Godfrey* character, but both LaCava and Hawks had the actress draw on her eccentric nature for these screwball roles. LaCava's name for his casual method, "go-as-you-please," also doubles as a further explanation as to why the director and Lombard were so close; both were fiercely independent.[12]

Lombard did face challenges during the *Godfrey* shoot. Most specifically, she spent hours in front of the mirror trying to find an appropriately zany look to match the zany dialogue her character spouted. At first thinking she "would go mad" before finding the expression, the actress later observed, "By letting my lips hang open just a trifle, widening my eyes and elevating the eyebrows, I managed to . . . [visually] fit Irene's habit of greeting the most obvious facts . . . with breathless surprise and delight."[13]

"Surprise and delight" would also be an apt description for the rave reviews *Godfrey* generated. Given Lombard's special preparation for the part, the *New York Times*'s affectionately amusing description of her character merits noting: "There is Irene, the cow-eyed, who has a one-track mind with grass growing over its rails."[14] More to the point, however, was the *New York Herald Tribune*'s review opening: "[Novelist] Eric Hatch's tale of a scavenger hunt, a goofy family and a blueblood butler [Powell] has been shaped to a lunatic and hilarious screen farce."[15] But given Lombard's love of baseball, she was probably most taken with *Variety*'s comparison of her character to an earlier era's screwball pitcher: "Miss Lombard has played screwball dames before, but none so screwy as this one . . . she needs only a resin bag to be a female Rube Waddell."[16]

Both the film and Lombard's performance generated

comparisons to two of her friends, *We're Not Dressing* (1934) costars George Burns and Gracie Allen, forever famous for their double-talk routines. Thus, the *New York Sun* called *Godfrey* "as goofy as a Burns and Allen conversation, which it somewhat resembles," while the *New York Evening Journal* stated with entertaining succinctness, "Miss Lombard goes completely Gracie Allen here."[17] (It's unknown whether Lombard called upon a Burns and Allen connection for her characterization, and it remains for future screwball comedy scholarship to explore these period parallels between the genre and this comedy team.) Ironically, as the *Hollywood Reporter* review stated, *Godfrey* was so well-received that "a good third of the dialogue is lost in continuous roars of audience laughter."[18]

What is forgotten today is the movie's significance to screwball comedy. Unlike any of the genre's predecessors, including the zany *Twentieth Century*, *Godfrey* offered a full menu of screwballs. Thus, for many 1930s critics, the latter film represented a more obvious starting point for the genre. For example, Kate Cameron's 1938 *New York Daily News* review of the classic screwball comedy *Bringing Up Baby* (1938) placed it in the tradition of "the whole crazy variety of screen comedies that began with 'My Man Godfrey.'"[19] Moreover, the greatest film critic of the 1930s, the *New Republic*'s Otis Ferguson, credited the movie with being the first to rate the screwball label. "With 'My Man Godfrey' in the middle of 1936, the discovery of the word screwball . . .

helped build the thesis of an absolutely new style in comedy," Ferguson noted.[20]

In addition to garnering critical acclaim and being a commercial success, *Godfrey* presented Lombard with her first and only Oscar nomination. Interestingly, one of Lombard's competitors for the Academy Award was fellow Hoosier Irene Dunne, who was nominated for another screwball comedy, *Theodora Goes Wild* (1936). The other actresses in the race were Gladys George for *Valiant Is the Word for Carrie*, Norma Shearer for *Romeo and Juliet*, and Luise Rainer for *The Great Ziegfeld*. The ultimate winner was Rainer, who won again the following year for *The Good Earth*. Rainer's first win has been tainted, however, by rumors that Louis B. Mayer delivered MGM's sizable block of votes to her. Be that as it may, Lombard was pleased to finally receive validation from the Motion Picture Academy. She had come a long way from that early label of merely a beautiful clotheshorse. Of equal importance to the blue-collar Lombard was another recognition she received from *Godfrey*. When the picture finished, all the production people presented "her with an enormous china egg, autographed and decorated until it looked like the egg that hatched the golden goose." It was punningly inscribed, "To Carole, a Good Egg."[21]

Sadly, Lombard's magical 1936 was marred by the death of another young Hollywood luminary, MGM's "boy genius" producer Irving Thalberg. His 14 September 1936 death at age thirty-seven nearly paralleled the opening of *Godfrey*. While Lombard knew Thalberg, his death affected her more by way of its impact on Gable. The fabled producer had acted as a major sponsor of Gable's early career, casting the actor opposite Thalberg's wife, Norma Shearer, in Gable's breakout movie, *A Free Soul* (1931). Thalberg cemented Gable's early success by casting him with Garbo in *Susan Lenox, Her Fall and Rise* (1931). Not surprisingly, the funeral of Thalberg, who was the catalyst for celebrated novelist F. Scott Fitzgerald's *The Last Tycoon* (1941), was a major filmland event, with Gable serving as an usher. Lombard was surprised that the actor seemed to be unmoved by Thalberg's death. Unlike Lombard, Gable was able to shut off his emotions, if he so desired.

Ironically, Lombard's extreme dislike for Thalberg's widow, Shearer, had reached a boiling point earlier in 1936. Carole had been responsible, in part, for organizing Hollywood's annual Mayfair Ball, which benefited the Motion Picture Relief Fund. The Mayfair Ball had a formal white dress code. All the guests complied save Shearer, who arrived in a bright crimson gown. This defiance made Lombard see her own special shade of red, seething to anyone within hearing distance, "Who the fuck does she think she is, the house madam?" Some might say this was hypocritical of Lombard, given her own tendency to tweak convention. But the difference was that Carole's iconoclasm was comic and creatively within the rules, such as her hospital white take on the Whitney party (see previous chapter). In contrast, Shearer's crimson entrance was purely an elitist power play that said, "My husband is the great Thalberg, and I don't have to play by the rules."

The incident entered Hollywood legend and, as is often the case in the film capital, it was soon recycled back into the movies. Two years later Betty Davis, wearing a shocking red dress, made an entrance to a southern ball in *Jezebel* (1938). The performance won Davis her second Academy Award. Through the years other directors have appropriated a similar dress-code violation for their films, such as Robert Altman having Cher wear red to a black-tie function in *The Player* (1992).

Returning to the original Shearer incident, Lombard might also have been irritated because this pompous showboating occurred at a charity event. Even though Lombard often attempted to avoid taking credit for charitable acts, she was always dead serious about them. One example of the actress's generosity that did not escape reporters, however, was her interceding on behalf of studio gaffer (electrician) Pat Drew.[22] Drew had lost a leg in a mid-1930s plane crash and had trouble getting work. Lombard had it put in her contract that Drew would help crew any picture she made, or she would walk off the set.

Another example of Lombard's beneficence mixed compassion with her love of tennis. One of the period's potentially great players, Alice Marble, contracted tuberculosis. While recuperating in a sanitarium, Marble became despondent

ALLEN COUNTY–FORT WAYNE HISTORICAL SOCIETY

*Lombard was Hollywood's most accomplished tennis player in the
1930s—a passion only rivaled by her love of animals.*

and let both her weight and complexion go. The actress
helped change Marble's life, starting with the following note:
"You don't know me but your tennis teacher is my teacher
and she has told me all about you. It really makes very little
difference who I am but once I thought I had a great career
in front of me, just like you thought you had. Then one day I
was in a terrible automobile accident. . . . Doctors told me I
was through. . . . Well—I proved them wrong . . . just as you
can—if you fight."[23]

Once out of the sanitarium, Marble was reborn via the
assistance of the actress and a team of doctors. Finding she

had been misdiagnosed, Marble was soon back playing tennis, losing weight, and being treated for acne. As Marble's life started to come together, Lombard believed the athlete needed to know more about clothes, so she had Marble take a University of Southern California class in costume design. Not only did Lombard pay all of Marble's medical and education expenses, but she also sponsored Marble in tournament play at a time when women tennis players had little commercial value. Marble, who later won Wimbledon, noted, "Every time I tried to pay her back she said, 'Oh, shit, forget about it.' She was always embarrassed when people wanted to thank her."[24]

Marble and Gable had something in common in 1936. Though they both dearly loved Lombard they were unhappy with the entourage of sycophants who frequently circled the star. This situation was an outgrowth of both the actress's generosity and a tendency on weekends to open her home to her mother and Bessie Peters's occult friends. The menagerie might include numerologists, mind readers, glad-hand types out for help, Lombard's gay tennis instructor, Madalynne Fields (her best friend and private secretary), brothers Fred and Stuart Peters, Hoosier visitors, and an army of other individuals just passing through. (Despite Lombard's heterosexual activity, the actress's masculine-like outspokenness and a live-in Fields had mid-1930s Hollywood gossips whispering that she was gay.) Over time Gable eventually weaned Lombard away from this exhausting entourage. However, it seemed a change the actress was ready to make, just as she scaled back her major party tendencies after 1936.

As if wanting to put her own distinctive stamp on the year, Lombard legally changed her name from Jane Peters Powell to Carole Lombard. Press coverage declared "that the name Carole Lombard was valuable to her from a business standpoint and she wished to protect it through the court action."[25] A celebrity renowned for eccentricity came into her own as a performer. Along related lines, a 1936 *Hollywood Reporter* poll credited Lombard with being a top box-office draw (Gable led all men; Shearer topped the women).[26] While this seems like merely stating the obvious, Lombard had never finished among the annual top ten box-office stars, according to the designated pollers, Quigley Publications.[27]

Without casting aspersions on the Quigley poll, the fact that Lombard had six consecutive critical and commercial hits in 1936 and 1937 alone (including *Godfrey* and *Swing High, Swing Low,* which was Paramount's top grosser for 1937) suggests that something was amiss in box-office coverage for Lombard. Thus, the *Hollywood Reporter's* 1936 poll constitutes an often neglected but still significant asterisk to the Quigley norm, with regard to Lombard. By taking the top fifty money-drawing names in the industry, the *Reporter* demonstrates Lombard's box-office clout. Though ranked just out of the top ten in the *Reporter* poll, Lombard was well ahead of such other prominent period actresses as Janet Gaynor, Marlene Dietrich, Bette Davis, Jean Harlow, and Katharine Hepburn. Interestingly enough, press coverage of the *Reporter* poll often implied that Lombard was a top-ten draw.[28]

Of all these footnotes to 1936, the budding romance with Gable easily takes the brass ring as Lombard's most memorable event. But she was not the only person in her circle to fall in love during 1936. Fields, her best friend from Mack Sennett days, had fallen in love with director Walter Lang, who had directed Lombard in both *No More Orchids* (1932) and *Love before Breakfast* (1936). Fields's marriage to Lang resulted in her retirement as Lombard's secretary. But the timing was good, given Lombard's new preoccupation with Gable, and Fields's mild disapproval of him as a man who she believed needed too much maintenance for any relationship.

The oddest Lombard-related headline of 1936, "Carole Lombard's Jewels for Sale," probably had a tie-in with Gable, too. The story quoted the actress as saying, "I just got tired of them," referring to her $50,000 collection of star sapphires.[29] Although the actress may well have lost interest in the jewels, the sale typified Lombard's simplification of her life after beginning her relationship with Gable. Lombard may have used the cash for the more secluded residence that allowed Gable to come and go discreetly. (Though separated from his second wife, Rhea Langham, Gable was still married when he began his romance with Lombard.) It did not take long, however, for the word to get out. *Liberty* magazine published, "Is Carole Lombard in Love at Last?" (1936), which chronicled the actress's many past romances and documented her liaison with Gable.[30] There was never any scandal attached to their relationship until a January 1939 *Photoplay* exposé titled "Hollywood's Unmarried Husbands and Wives." The article, which will be addressed at greater length later, examined several couples living as husband and wife but without benefit of a marriage certificate.[31] Many of the couples featured, including Lombard and Gable, fearing an ethical backlash at the box office, made their relationships legal.

In 1936, however, the biggest threat to the budding romance of Lombard and Gable was their busy film schedules. While Lombard had three pictures released in 1936, no less than four new Gable movies appeared, including the critical and commercial hit *San Francisco*, which costarred his friend Spencer Tracy. After Shirley Temple, Gable was the top box-office draw of the 1930s, and MGM was maximizing its investment in its star.

As previously noted, Lombard often seemed to change more for the men in her life than they did for her. This pattern held for Gable, as she took up his twin passions of hunting and fishing. But Lombard was not without her victories. Her new lover had a reputation for frugality. This was most markedly brought home to Lombard at the wrap party for *Love on the Run* (1936). The crew had displayed gifts given by Gable's costars, his former lover Joan Crawford and her then husband Franchot Tone. Lombard did some quick research and discovered that her man never gave production presents. Gable blamed it on the no-gift tradition he had

observed early in his MGM career; presents were never policy with stars such as Garbo and Wallace Beery.[32] Carole
changed Gable's policy, putting herself in charge of all his
future wrap-party gifts but billing him for the service.

Although Gable had always had a healthy sense of
humor, he soon discovered that a person needed a very thick
skin to cope with Lombard. She was an unmerciful kidder
and practical joker, from her gift of a ham emblazoned with
his picture upon the completion of 1932's *No Man of Her
Own* (a photographer was on hand to record the gag), to a
litany of private jabs at such things as his ears, his false teeth,
his virility, the greater popularity of Temple, and his stingy
tendencies. Gable not only seemed to enjoy such kidding, he
also often shared her wicked sense of humor with others.

Gable even got a laugh out of a Lombard prank that targeted one of the actor's rare 1930s film failures, *Parnell*
(1937), a biography of a popular late-nineteenth-century
Irish nationalist whose political career was ruined by an affair
with a married woman. Gable had an aversion to playing historical figures, preferring to portray contemporary versions of
himself. Using the argument that these prestigious profiles
were often popular with the public, MGM brass convinced
Gable to take the part. The problem with *Parnell* was that the
character was less than dynamic, and, to make matters worse,
exited with a milquetoast death scene. In prewar Hollywood
a Garbo or a Beery might die. Indeed, James Cagney made
the drawn out death scene an art form. Once Gable moved

beyond his early gangster roles, however, it was forbidden that his character die, at least until *Parnell*. Needless to say, critics and fans alike panned the movie, and Gable did not die on screen again for more than twenty years, in 1958's *Run Silent, Run Deep*.

Lombard hired a pilot to fly over the studio at Culver City and drop thousands of leaflets with the title, "Fifty Million Chinamen Can't Be Wrong!" Comically, this was a reference to a rare positive *Parnell* review from, of all places, a Chinese source. Nothing if not thorough, Lombard also had part of the review reproduced on the leaflets. Gable was immensely amused, but MGM was not. Among the couple's friends the leaflet drop was sometimes known as "Carole's Rain of Terror." What else could one expect from Hollywood's reigning eccentric? Both privately and professionally, 1936 had been the best of years for her. More major successes loomed on the horizon.

8

Encore

When one character in Nothing Sacred *observes, "For good
clean fun there's nothing like a wake," Lombard's supposedly
dying character replys, "Oh please, let's not talk shop."*

IF CAROLE LOMBARD'S MEMORABLE 1936 IS LIKENED TO A HIT
play, the year 1937 was an encore performance. In addition
to her continued romance with Clark Gable, Lombard once
again had three critical and commercial hits—*Swing High,
Swing Low*; *Nothing Sacred*; and *True Confession*. Also, as in
1936 with *My Man Godfrey*, one of her 1937 films, *Nothing
Sacred*, is now considered a classic.

Lombard's first 1937 film, *Swing High, Swing Low*, was
a mix of comedy and drama that impressed critics with its
ability to blend genres. *New York Post* critic Archer Winsten
waxed poetic on this phenomenon, noting the movie opening
"by starting off with a high comic bang and ending up in the
low register of sobs and pathos."[1] *New York American* reviewer Robert Garland described the film as "Garnished . . . with
girls and glamour, merriment and music, the tenant of the . . .
[film] remains essentially a romance."[2] (The property was
adapted from the play *Burlesque*, which had been filmed in

1929 as *Dance of Life*.)

The movie, which teamed for the third time Lombard and Fred MacMurray, is essentially a romantic comedy that slides into melodrama, chronicling the relationship of two cabaret performers. Set in Panama and New York, the movie has Lombard playing singer Maggie King, and MacMurray is trumpeter Skid Johnson. King helps make a musical career happen for Skid, who is just out of the army. He eventually graduates to the big time (New York) and promises to send for her. But success and another singer (Dorothy Lamour in her second picture) prove too distracting. Later, when Maggie's career also brings her to New York, Skid realizes the error of his ways. As with most melodramatic plot twists, however, instead of communicating with his now estranged lover, Skid lives up to his nickname, embraces his guilt, and allows his life and career to implode. But at the eleventh hour Maggie rescues his career and, presumably, their relationship.

As with most performers, Lombard's choice of her favorite film role fluctuated over time, but she frequently selected Maggie King, often in close competition with Irene Bullock (from *Godfrey*) and Hazel Flagg (from *Nothing Sacred*). Although Lombard's brimming with moxie Maggie is a charming character, *Swing High, Swing Low* is not in a class with her other two classic movies. Ironically, what pleased period critics and fans—the blending of film genres—proves to be a distraction for modern viewers and the genre switches seem arbitrary instead of story driven. Plus, the periodic transformations of MacMurray's character, such as his sudden self-destructive guilt, are seldom rooted in anything one has seen before in this character. The movie's director, Mitchell Leisen, later admitted that MacMurray doubted he could play the dramatic scenes.[3] Though Leisen believed that MacMurray was ultimately successful, part of the character's failure might be rooted in the actor's lack of dramatic range.

Whatever one's take on MacMurray's performance, his minimalist acting persona seemed more geared to comedy. Notwithstanding his later ability to play a heel (which is essentially what Skid Johnson is), especially in Billy Wilder's *Double Indemnity* (1944) and *The Apartment* (1960), MacMurray's stoical style probably helped enhance Lombard's gift for broad comedy. Most comedy teams are tied as much to contrasts in personality as any variation in size. For example, what best defines Laurel and Hardy is how Hardy's demonstrative style differs from Laurel's placid personality. Hardy's broadness is comically "lightened" by Laurel's delightful vacuousness. Or, to use *New Yorker* critic John Lahr's poetic metaphor, "Light needs shadow to intensify its brilliance."[4]

Though one might not normally associate the personality comedian, à la Laurel and Hardy, with the romantic and/or screwball comedy couple, the same contrast in personalities might apply. For example, *My Man Godfrey* is driven by the comic difference between screwball Lombard and normal William Powell. *Variety*'s review of the picture inadvertently addresses this variation in its praise of Lombard, noting "Miss

Lombard's role is the more difficult . . . since it calls for pressure acting [ongoingly zany] all the way. . . . It's Powell's job to be normal and breezily comic in the madcap household [of Lombard], and that doesn't require stretching for him."[5]

One of the challenges for Leisen on *Swing High, Swing Low*, and presumably when he directed Lombard and MacMurray in *Hands Across the Table* (1935), was that Lombard was "at her best on the first take . . . [and] Fred MacMurray often needed the first couple of takes to get into the swing of it."[6] Leisen's secret for keeping Lombard's performance fresh was to either give her new physical bits of business to do each take, or to give a green light to her natural flair for improvisation. Leisen also allowed MacMurray, who was still evolving as an actor, to put scripted dialogue in his own words, if that would make it easier for him. This gave Lombard's performance a realistically edgy tone because she did not always have set script cues to respond to. Consequently, while *Swing High, Swing Low* only had intermittent moments of screwball comedy, the film often had the off-the-cuff ambience of that genre.

As a footnote of interest, *Swing*'s New York opening at the Paramount Theatre featured Louis Armstrong and his band as the stage show between screenings of the picture. It was a natural connection given that Armstrong was a trumpeter credited with establishing the preeminence of the virtuoso jazz soloist, and MacMurray's *Swing* role was a jazz trumpeter prone to solo riffs, which were dubbed for the actor.

New York Evening Journal critic Rose Pelswick credited the combination of Lombard, MacMurray, and Armstrong with creating fan pandemonium at the *Swing* opening. "Judging by the crowds that packed the house at yesterday's first performance," Pelswick wrote, "the new show is set for several weeks."[7]

Before closing the book on *Swing*, a final example of Lombard's generosity as a performer merits noting. The actress took an instant liking to newcomer Dorothy Lamour, and not only had Lamour's part enhanced, but also protected the nervous young actress when mistakes were made. Lamour later remembered, "On our first scene together, I blew my lines over and over. Carole always knew her lines perfectly but she began to blow them on purpose just so I wouldn't feel bad!"[8] Anthony Quinn, who had a miniscule part in *Swing* (quite possibly arranged by Lombard), had already been befriended by Lombard before the production began. He was impressed by both her egalitarian attitude and the actress's no-nonsense nature, such as her thoughts on Quinn's marriage to the daughter of celebrated director Cecil B. DeMille: "Son-in-laws have a rough time in this town. First there are the ass-kissers who will try to use you to get to the Old Man, and then there are the guys who will try to knock you down to get even with him. You're going to get it coming and going."[9]

Lombard's movie career was in high gear. *Swing* was followed by one of American film's watershed works, the screwball classic *Nothing Sacred*. It remains entertaining today, in part because the story is anchored in dark comedy. Lombard's character, Hazel Flagg, is a small-town girl allegedly dying of radium poisoning. Fredric March plays a New York reporter who hatches a publicity gimmick in which his newspaper will bankroll an all-expense-paid visit to the city for Flagg in exchange for the exclusive rights to her tragic story. Where's the humor in that? Well, Lombard's character is not really at death's door, but only she and her small-town doctor (Charles Winninger) know the truth. Winninger, aptly named Dr. Enoch Downer, originally had misdiagnosed Hazel, possibly because he was also the village's alcoholic veterinarian! The duo of Downer and Flagg decide, however, to cash in on this free New York extravaganza. (Downer's accompaniment is essential to maintaining Flagg's cover.)

As noted earlier, screwball comedy is often laced with a generous slice of satire, and *Nothing Sacred* scriptwriter Ben Hecht is more than up to the task here. Thus, while Hecht and Charles MacArthur had targeted the theater in their screenplay for *Twentieth Century* (1934, adapted from their play), Hecht undercuts the world of big-city journalism in *Nothing Sacred*. Fittingly, Dr. Downer had been wronged years before in a newspaper contest by March's fictional *New York Morning Star*. This allows Winninger's physician both a reason for maintaining a lie about Lombard's character and an excuse to periodically tee off at journalism: "I'll tell you briefly what I think of newspaper men. The hand of God reaching down into the mire couldn't elevate one of 'em to the depths of degradation!" But a sideswiping of journalism is not limited to Winninger. Even March's reporter, Wally Cook, gets into the act, such as his description of his editor as "a cross between a Ferris wheel and a werewolf."

Lombard is part of the satirical equation in two ways. First, she plays a small-town girl capable of turning the tables on the obsequious Manhattanites. Instead of being suckered by the city (the normal turn of events), Hazel, as the original ads proclaimed, "took New York for a sleigh ride." Film comedy historian James Harvey has likened this aspect of the film to the *Catcher in the Rye* world of Holden Caulfield—New York: "the place is full of phonies."[10] Surprisingly, however, the movie does not play homage to small-town life; *Nothing Sacred* targets it as well. Hazel takes advantage of the free trip to New York because she hates life in her village. Similar to Lombard's character in *No Man of Her Own* (1932), Flagg will do anything to leave her tiny community. As she explains her tears to Dr. Downer, after he tells her she is not going to die of radium poisoning, "It's kind of startling to be brought to life twice—and each time in [small town] Warsaw."

For 1930s viewers, *Nothing Sacred*'s satirical rendering of small-town life had a more focused target—director Frank Capra's America, as personified by his critical and commercial hit *Mr. Deeds Goes to Town* (1936). In an interview with *Nothing Sacred* director William Wellman, he shared that it was always fun tweaking Capra, his friendly rival.[11] Wally's

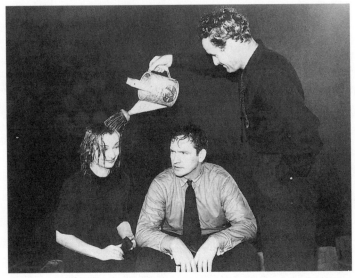

THE MUSEUM OF MODERN ART/FILM STILL ARCHIVES

Director William Wellman waters down Nothing Sacred *(1937) stars Lombard and Fredric March for the fake suicide scene.*

visit to Warsaw to make his offer to Hazel parallels the open-ing of *Mr. Deeds* when Gary Cooper's small-town character is visited by New Yorkers anxious to bring him back to the city. But whereas Capra makes his village inhabitants merely eccentric, *Nothing Sacred* treats them as comic opportunists ("I wouldn'ta talked at all if I knew I was gonna do it for noth-ing") and potentially lethal (a small boy on all fours darts out of one yard and bites Wally on the leg).

Notwithstanding these satirical targets, to qualify as screwball comedy a movie also needs to spoof the world of

romantic comedy, and *Nothing Sacred* excels in this department. Where a normal romance features a sensitive
courtship, circumstances necessitate that both Hazel and
Wally take turns socking one another. Indeed, promotional
material for the picture frequently pictured them in a boxing
ring, and critics sometimes carried the analogy into their
reviews. For example, *New York Journal American* critic
Regina Crewe opened her review with, "It's a K.O. [knock
out] comedy at the Music Hall."[12]

Nothing Sacred's take off on romance was also tied to its
dark-comedy component, such as Wally's slant on the chancy
nature of marrying Hazel. It would be "like honeymooning
with the hearse at the front door." This is hardly the poetic
small talk featured in a true love story. Plus, screwball comedy
invariably kids romance by making the heroine eccentrically
dominant over the leading man. This is certainly the case
throughout *Nothing Sacred*. Even near the film's close, when
Hazel plans to fake a watery suicide and Wally attempts to save
her, he forgets that he cannot swim! The "drowning" Hazel has
to save him. This difference in dominance is further height-
ened by the contrasting personae of Lombard and March. As
with the variation between MacMurray and Lombard, March
finds himself playing straight man to the actress.

This David O. Selznick production was a monster critical
success, which was further assisted by being in Technicolor.
(Out of the hundreds of feature films released in 1937, only
six were in Technicolor.) Other than some random early

Technicolor sequences in her Mack Sennett silent-short days, this was Lombard's first and only Technicolor film. And to use a 1930s colloquialism, Lombard in color was so lovely everyone wanted a "look see." *Variety's* rave review managed to salute this fact, and nearly everything else about *Nothing Sacred*: "The stock of Carole Lombard will be helped by the picture. . . . The comedy is as cleverly produced as it's written and acted, while for added value there is . . . Technicolor which greatly enhances its pictorial charm."[13]

Despite *Nothing Sacred's* period critical acclaim and the movie's current status as a classic, the decidedly lesser *Swing High, Swing Low* proved to be a bigger box-office hit. The explanation is undoubtedly in the old axiom, "satire doesn't play well on Saturday night," at least in the smaller and less sophisticated markets. Plus, *Nothing Sacred's* dark-comedy strain, which paradoxically makes the movie seem so contemporary, probably initially worked against it in rural areas and in small towns (Capra country). Even several large-market publications reacted with surprise at some of the picture's dark-comedy themes, such as the omnipresence of death. For example, Kate Cameron's otherwise positive *New York Daily News* review stated, "when the movies can kid anything as solemn as death . . . as an incitation to laughter, nothing in life IS sacred."[14]

All things considered, however, *Nothing Sacred* was a modest commercial hit. If overall box-office returns were disappointing, there was the prestige of being held over for three weeks at Radio City Music Hall, America's premier movie venue. What made the movie more popular than, for example, the earlier satirical screwball comedy *Twentieth Century*, was that one of its key targets (New York) was a subject that America's hinterland loved to hate. The *Oklahoma News* had the following praise for *Nothing Sacred*, "So please take our word for it that you'll have one long laugh from the time this [opening] foreword is flashed on the screen, 'New York, where truth, crushed to earth, rises again as phony as a glass eye.'"[15]

Ticket sales were no doubt also assisted by entertaining comic stories associated with the movie's production, such as *Life* magazine crediting director Wellman with the belief "that the way to get a cast into the spirit of a farce is to create the general atmosphere of a lunatic asylum [on the set]."[16] (Lombard and March eventually presented Wellman with a straitjacket.) Obviously playing upon the party atmosphere Gregory LaCava had created for *My Man Godfrey*, Wellman later footnoted the connection by telling Carole that he "liked Gregory LaCava's comedies much better [than *Nothing Sacred*]."[17] But this might have been partially dictated by the fact that Wellman had less opportunity than LaCava to improvise because Hecht's pricey, high-profile script was nearly sacred.

Nothing Sacred was still playing in many markets when *True Confession*, Lombard's third 1937 critical and commercial hit, opened. Its release late in the year gave *New York Times* critic Frank S. Nugent the opportunity to use the hol-

WES D. GEHRING

Lombard plays at being a murderer in True Confession
(1937, with Fred MacMurray).

iday season as a fitting time to celebrate Lombard's body of work for the year. The lengthy punning title for his article might also double as its synopsis, "A CHRISTMAS CAROLE: Being a Tardy Salute to Miss Lombard, One of Our Brightest Comediennes."[18]

Critics found parallels between *True Confession* and *Nothing Sacred* as both were screwball comedies with dark-comedy overtones and each starred Lombard. In *True Confessions* Lombard teamed once again with MacMurray. The movie was reminiscent of their *The Princess Comes Across* (1936), as each of these skewerings of romantic comedy mixes murder with merriment. In *True Confession,* Lombard plays the wife of a defense lawyer (MacMurray) so honest that he can find few clients he trusts. In contrast, Lombard's character, Helen Bartlett, is a congenital liar, a forerunner of Goldie Hawn's inventive liar in *Housesitter* (1992). With no money coming in, Helen is forced to take a secretarial job with a wealthy businessman. When he makes a pass at her, she walks out on him. Returning later for her hat, coat, and purse, she finds the boss murdered. Helen soon becomes the prime suspect. Deciding to go with her natural flair for lying, Helen hatches a whopper, claiming she murdered her boss when he attempted to take advantage of her. The beauty of the plan is that it also provides her husband with his big chance to win a high-profile acquittal and make his career. The trial also provided this screwball comedy with its primary satirical target, the law.

If possible, the reviews for *True Confession* were even stronger than the critiques of *Nothing Sacred*. The *New York Times* credited the film with being "a highly polished, smoothly grained Yule log which deserves to crackle right merrily at the Paramount [theater] from now until well after

Christmas."[19] *New York Daily Mirror* critic Bland Johaneson comically observed, "Miss Lombard's latest excursion into the region of Dim Wits . . . is a gem of hilarity."[20] *New York Daily News* reviewer Kate Cameron noted that Lombard both, "proves once more that she is one of the greatest comediennes," as well as giving a classic "tongue-in-cheek" performance.[21] (The "cheek" reference was a celebration of Lombard's *True Confession* tendency to roll her tongue around in her mouth just prior to telling a tall tale.)

As entertaining as Lombard is in the film, John Barrymore steals the show as a psychopathic alcoholic who confesses to the murder because he resents Lombard's liar getting all the attention. Thus, while the *New York Herald Tribune* described the actor's performance as a "tour-de-force of farcical make-believe," the *New York World-Telegram* critic stated, "the chief joy of the offering is John Barrymore's impersonation of a liquor-sodden, slightly daft . . . [criminologist]. Here is a grand piece of acting, worthy of a film that is the greatest fun."[22] Barrymore's usurping of critical attention would not have pleased most stars, but Lombard was happy for her buddy and mentor. Her old costar's career had been in decline, relegating him to B-movie roles. Lombard thought that *True Confession* had a small but provocative part just right for a Barrymore comeback. To pad her hunch, however, she had the film's screenwriter, her friend Claude Binyon, enhance Barrymore's role. The mutual-admiration society that was Lombard and Barrymore was nicely demon-

WES D. GEHRING

This True Confession *moment (with MacMurray) was very much how America saw Lombard—the nonstop free spirit.*

strated later when *Time* magazine suggested the actor had stolen the film, to which Barrymore responded, "Nobody ever steals a picture from Carole Lombard."[23]

Between her high-visibility career and personal relationship with Gable, Lombard was frequently in the news during 1937, forming a pattern for the rest of her life. Lombard had always been good at generating publicity via her gags, parties, and quips, but press space came even easier now. Though usually of a positive sort, there were some distractions, such as the noisy Missouri tourists who interrupted the shooting of a scene on the set of *True Confession*. The actress cut loose with language so blue that a "distraught assistant director scurried up waving his arms: 'Please, Miss Lombard, please! Remember there are ladies present.'"[24]

Other 1937 Lombard news events of merit range from the Academy Awards banquet at the Los Angeles Biltmore Hotel (4 March), to the announcement by Selznick International Pictures (10 December) that a bronze plaque was soon to be dedicated at 704 Rockhill Street, the actress's Fort Wayne birthplace.[25] At the Academy Awards, Luise Rainer took home the Best Actress Oscar, with Lombard's *Godfrey* performance finishing a close second. (Presenter George Jessel revealed the voting breakdown, which was not unusual for 1930s Oscar ceremonies.) Lombard and Gable attended the event with ex-husband Powell (also nominated for *Godfrey*) and his fiancée Jean Harlow. Sadly, the next occasion to bring the foursome together would be Harlow's funeral on 9 June. (Harlow's death was attributed to uremic poisoning). Lombard and her friend Madalynne Fields spent a great deal of time with Powell in the weeks after Harlow's death trying to help him cope with the loss. It was no easy task, especially since Lombard and Gable also had been close to the actress.

The placement of a historic marker at Lombard's home in Fort Wayne was a happy distraction. It was touted at the time as an unprecedented honor for a motion picture performer. Though originally orchestrated by Selznick Pictures, the implementation of the award was soon turned over to Fort Wayne officials.[26] In the end, both Selznick and the city benefited. The film company received added publicity for the Fort Wayne opening of *Nothing Sacred*, which occurred shortly after the plaque dedication (1 January 1938), and the city was able to salute its most famous performer. Hoosier legend maintains that Lombard ruffled local feathers by initially agreeing to attend the dedication, only to pull out in order to go on a hunting trip with Gable.[27] Close scrutiny of Fort Wayne's period newspapers reveals no reference to such a commitment from the actress. These same publications, however, document that Lombard followed the proceedings with great interest and pride. For example, the finished bronze plaque was first sent to Hollywood so she could sign off on the wording. Lombard was so pleased with the results that she had her photograph taken with the marker and included it in the return shipment of the plaque "to show to

W. C. Fields on the set of his Poppy *(1936), the
same year as* My Man Godfrey.

her many friends in Fort Wayne her appreciation."[28] On the eve of the ceremony, Lombard telegraphed Fort Wayne Mayor Harry W. Baals: "It is good to know you are remembered in your own hometown. I am grateful to the people of Fort Wayne for this honor and I am especially grateful to you. I wish I could be present to express my delighted appreciation in a more emphatic manner. Best wishes for the New Year to you all."[29]

Lombard's high visibility in 1937 also made her the target of a scam-artist ring. During the Christmas holidays, several stars, including Lombard, Claudette Colbert, and Joan Crawford, received "begging letters" from fake relatives. In Lombard's case, the Fort Wayne postmarked letter said, in part, "I am sure you would not want to know that a member of your family is on [government] relief."[30] Her alleged relative asked for $500. (No arrests were made in the Lombard case.)

Ironically, the most impressive Lombard inspired news item of 1937 did not actually carry the actress's name. W. C. Fields, celebrated comedian and drinking buddy of *Godfrey* director LaCava, was irked that the Academy Awards ceremony once again had neglected comedy and the unique status of *Godfrey*. Failure of the film's four nominated performers (Lombard, Powell, and supporting actors Alice Brady and Mischa Auer) to take home an Oscar was the catalyst for his following remarks: "Any actor knows that comedy is more difficult, requires more artistry, than any other form of acting. It is pretty easy to fool an audience with a little crepe hair and a dialect but . . . [comedy] is either funny or . . . [not] . . . . This isn't a case of sour grapes with me, because I didn't grow any grapes last year. I didn't even sow a wild oat."[31]

Unlike Fields's comically flippant close to his remarks, Lombard was more than a little upset at not winning an Oscar. Moreover, given that Gable had already taken home a statuette for *It Happened One Night* (1934), the forever competitive Lombard was also anxious to match him. The fact that she never even received another nomination qualified her for a legitimate case of sour grapes.

9

Clark Gable and *Gone with the Wind*

Lombard "gets up too early, plays tennis too hard, wastes time and feelings on trifles and drinks Coca-Colas the way Samuel Johnson used to drink tea. She is a scribbler on telephone pads, inhibited nail-biter . . . and chain cigarette smoker. When . . . [she] talks, her conversation, often brilliant, is punctured by screeches, laughs, growls, gesticulations and the expletives of a sailor's parrot."[1]

IN 1938 CAROLE LOMBARD CHANGED HER PRIORITIES. FOR THE first time in her life she put a man ahead of her movie career. Only one new Lombard picture, *Fools for Scandal*, was released in 1938, with part of that film shot in late 1937. In the previous two years she had made six films, while in the first half of the 1930s Lombard had averaged a whopping five films a year. Clark Gable or no Clark Gable, it was probably a good time for a breather. Moreover, competing film production schedules had torpedoed her relationship with William Powell, and she told herself this would not happen with Gable.

Lombard threw herself into Gable's twin passions of hunting and fishing, often being the only woman along on these normally all-male outings. In Gable's favor, however, he never imposed any "boys' night out" restrictions, welcoming her company if Lombard could keep up. Amusingly, she soon surpassed him. Lombard told Garson Kanin, "The only trouble is—about the shooting I mean—I've gotten to be so much better than he is that I've got to hold back. I can shoot like a sonofabitch, y'know."[2] But these hunting and fishing trips, when they traveled as just a couple, often also included more than a little sexual activity. Moreover, the easily bored Lombard was never averse to playing a sexy trump card, such as giving Clark some provocative additional options for that duck blind as opposed to just waiting. Make no mistake, while the actress was never afraid to rough it, she began each wilderness outing in tailored hunting and fishing apparel. As in her movies, she was never afraid to get messy, but Lombard started each adventure looking like a million dollars.

Lombard's period of transition was not dictated totally by Gable. The poor critical and commercial response to the March release of *Fools for Scandal* made Lombard rethink her screwball comedy film career. The genre had fueled her filmography for more than two years, but the movie's reception suggested Lombard had gone to the metaphorical well one time too many. The *New York Times* was the most entertainingly biting in its description of *Fools for Scandal*, noting that "the last dessicated shreds of comedy have been plucked from the bones of the [Gregory] LaCava masterpiece [1936's *My Man Godfrey*], and an east wind blows dismally through its skeleton."[3]

Despite the film's overall negative reception, the ever-popular Lombard seemed criticism proof. The *New York*

Herald Tribune observed, "Although it has Carole Lombard working overtime to achieve a clowning mood . . . it is a witless, wearisome entertainment."[4] Though *Fools for Scandal* was not without its period champions (*Variety* credited the film with "many diverting moments"[5]), the *New York Daily News*'s casually comic take on the film was probably closer to the truth: "I'm not going to be the one to advise you to drop everything this week to rush and see [*Fools for Scandal*]."[6] Not surprisingly, Lombard's friends described her as being "shellshocked" by the film's disappointing reception.[7] Lombard was nothing if not resilient, and she coped by focusing her energies on making her relationship with Gable work.

One could argue that even if Lombard had had a stronger screwball comedy property, it might not have found an audience in 1938. This was the year the genre was said to hit the proverbial wall. No less a classic than *Bringing Up Baby* (1938, with Cary Grant and Katharine Hepburn) proved to be a disappointment at the box office. Needless to say, Lombard believed it was time to return to straight drama, and in her next four films (1939–40) she did just that. Meanwhile, she took nearly a year off. (Ironically, it was at this time that *Life* magazine did its famous cover article on Lombard, "A Loud Cheer for the Screwball Girl."[8])

Working or not, Lombard, along with most other actresses in 1938, aspired to play Scarlet O'Hara in the film adaptation of the novel that had become a publishing phenomenon, *Gone with the Wind*. The Civil War saga stayed on the *New*

York Times's best-seller list for almost two consecutive years after its 1936 publication. David O. Selznick purchased the film rights, and Lombard hoped that her contractual ties to him, starting with *Nothing Sacred* (1937), would aid her in getting the role. Plus, to use a sports analogy the athletic Lombard might have appreciated, her career had peaked at the right time for serious consideration. Lombard, not above playing Hollywood politics, stayed with her often difficult agent, Myron Selznick, because he was David's brother.

Unfortunately, the fact that Gable was the public's choice to play Rhett Butler did not advance Lombard's case with David Selznick. If Gable was to be part of the package, something neither man initially favored, Lombard's chance to play Scarlet was hurt on several levels. First, according to Gable biographer Lyn Tornabene, Lombard believed that since she and Gable were openly living together (Gable was still married to second wife Rhea Langham), "Selznick wouldn't risk damaging his picture with pressure from inevitable groups of the morally outraged" if he cast both of them.[9]

From Selznick's perspective, a Gable-Lombard teaming had two additional liabilities. First, the producer was already afraid that his power base might be threatened by giving America's favorite actor the pivotal role of Rhett Butler. If Gable's lover (Lombard) was then given the plum part of Scarlet, Gable would have more leverage over the production. Selznick's second fear related to a Gable-Lombard teaming was that if the couple's personal relationship should for some

WES D. GEHRING

Gable's 1938 signing to star in Gone with the Wind *(1939), with David O. Selznick (center) and Louis B. Mayer.*

reason end prior to the movie's release, it would sour the public's response to the *Gone with the Wind* romance.

In addition to Gable and Selznick's mutual dislike for one another, the producer also resisted casting Gable because of the price demanded by the actor's parent studio, MGM. Louis B. Mayer, the head of MGM, demanded distribution rights and a percentage of the profits for the movie. Such an arrangement would cost independent producer Selznick millions, as well as delaying production because he was tied to a distribution deal with United Artists until 1939. The Mayer demand approached the level of extortion, especially given that he was also Selznick's father-in-law! Mayer knew that Gable had become equated with Rhett Butler in the reading public's collective consciousness. (A popular misperception is that Margaret Mitchell wrote the novel with Gable in mind. In fact, she had completed most of the book by 1931, the year that Gable's career took off.)

Despite Mayer's strong position, Selznick thought he had a way around it. The producer's correspondence documents that he believed Gary Cooper was an equally viable candidate to play Rhett Butler.[10] Knowing this, Lombard hatched what one Cooper biographer labeled her "bizarre plot" to capture the role of Scarlet.[11] Lombard was equally aware that Cooper did not want to play Rhett Butler, believing it was strictly a supporting role. She asked him, however, to tentatively accept the part so that a Paramount package for *Gone with the Wind* (including her as Scarlet) could be arranged. Then, if Cooper backed out of the project, Lombard reasoned that Mayer would acquiesce to loaning Gable at more favorable terms, given that a joint-distribution arrangement would have already been signed between Paramount and United Artists.

Bizarre or not, it might have worked had Cooper played along.

Ironically, Cooper might just as well have aided Lombard. Although he privately suggested he "wouldn't touch the role with a ten foot pole," Cooper's no to Selznick was so unconvincing that the producer was hopeful well into 1938 that he might still land the actor as Rhett Butler. Cooper's oscillation was fueled by both the huge popular success of the novel and his own personal rivalry with Gable. This latter point, as well as Cooper's doubts about the overblown, strife-ridden film adaptation of the novel, came out clearly in a statement he made to director William Wellman (*Beau Geste*, 1939) while both pictures were in production: "*Gone with the Wind* is going to be the biggest flop in Hollywood history. I'm just glad it'll be Clark Gable who's falling flat on his face and not Gary Cooper."[12]

Though Cooper's take on the picture might qualify as one of Hollywood's most misguided predictions, it was not far from Gable's own private fears. Since the *Parnell* (1937) fiasco, he had become almost paranoid about period costume films. Gable also feared disappointing the approximately six million people who had read *Gone with the Wind*: "It meant having everyone of them looking me in the eye and saying, 'You better be good, boy!'"[13] Unlike Cooper, however, Gable was in no position to refuse the role. Privately, the always movie savvy Lombard peppered him with the idea that this picture would be the crowning achievement of his career (which made her a better prognosticator than Cooper).

Professionally, Gable could not afford to say no to Selznick and Mayer because MGM would suspend him without pay. With an expensive and inevitable divorce from Langham looming ahead, he would need the studio's assistance in paying off his second wife.

Consequently, while Gable was amusingly on record as telling Selznick, "I don't want the part for money, chalk, or marbles," on 25 August 1938 the public learned that Gable would play Rhett Butler. It had been a foregone conclusion for months, and MGM and Mayer scored a monetary bonanza. For the loan of Gable and putting up half the production costs, approximately $3 million, MGM received half-ownership of the film for seven years and 25 percent thereafter. In addition, the studio received 50 percent of the film's gross profits. Because of the famous search for Scarlet, Gable was able to shoot *Idiot's Delight* (1939) before beginning *Gone with the Wind*. Gable biographer Charles Samuels credits the search with seeming "to keep the fans goggle-eyed with suspense."[14]

Despite the invaluable publicity it generated for the picture, the search was mostly a smoke screen, holding up production until an acceptable script was forthcoming and the Gable-Cooper question had been decided. (Another potential delay if MGM became part of the package was Selznick's contract to distribute all his pictures through United Artists until 1939.)

Nearly all of Hollywood's top actresses did screen tests

for Scarlet. Two of Lombard's favorite stories related to this competition involved Lucille Ball and Katharine Hepburn. A Lombard protégé, Ball, when asked to take a screen test, responded, "Me play Scarlett O'Hara? Are you kidding?" Hepburn, considered an early front-runner after her test, was ultimately rejected by Selznick because he could not see Gable pursuing her for almost four hours! Selznick was also well aware that Hepburn was considered "box-office poison" at the time.

Lombard still had not given up on capturing the role. When Selznick decided to produce *Made for Each Other* (1939) prior to *Gone with the Wind*, Lombard jumped at the chance to be in it. In addition to meeting her restricted work demand, only accepting roles that paralleled Gable assignments, she hoped to impress Selznick by excelling in this comedy drama. This sometimes melodramatic slice-of-life film involved the trying times of an underpaid attorney (Jimmy Stewart) and his wife (Lombard). The picture was a major critical success, with the actress scoring her best reviews for a mostly dramatic role. The *New York Journal American* observed, "It's Miss Lombard's first serious part after much too long a siege of wacky forces, and with her performance here she establishes herself as a dramatic actress of talent and distinction."[15] *New York World-Telegram* critic William Boehnel raved about the actress's work, "Carole Lombard turns in a performance as the young wife which will tear your heart to shreds. It is so sure and true, so completely good that

WES D. GEHRING

A melodramatic moment from Made for Each Other
(1939, with Jimmy Stewart).

it is beyond criticism."[16] *Variety's* rave review was typical of the critical consensus, "This is an exquisitely played, deeply moving comedy-drama. It is a happy combination of young love, sharp cleancut humor and tearjerker of the first water. David

182

O. Selznick's production leaves no sagging at the seams."[17]

Even before the film's release, Lombard's performance generated Oscar buzz in the industry, with the picture eventually being included in the *New York Times*'s prestigious "Ten Best" list for 1939.[18] This was no small accomplishment, given that 1939 is now considered the benchmark year for Hollywood's studio system. Obviously, her performance strengthened Lombard's case to play Scarlet. As late as December 1938 the *Hollywood Reporter* predicted that Lombard would win filmland's most coveted role.[19]

Though pleased with her acting in *Made for Each Other*, Lombard was bowled over by the work of her costar Stewart. Ever the generous colleague, she sang his praises to whoever would listen. Lombard lauded Stewart in a guest column she did for syndicated journalist Ed Sullivan (later famous for his television variety show). The following is an excerpt from that long-forgotten column: "If I were boss of Hollywood, Ed, there is one thing I would recommend for all young actors. I would tell them to get prints of Jimmy Stewart's motion pictures and take them home. I would advise them to run them off again and again, and to study them in the most minute detail. For perfection in timing, there isn't an actor in all Hollywood who tops Stewart. It is natural with him."[20] (Consistent with Lombard's praise, Stewart received an Oscar nomination for another of his 1939 films, the Frank Capra classic *Mr. Smith Goes to Washington*. The following year Stewart won an Academy Award as Best Actor for his performance in *The Philadelphia Story*.)

Prior to Lombard's February 1939 column on Stewart, she and Gable and several other unmarried couples were blindsided by a January *Photoplay* exposé, which hit news-stands over the holidays. With the provocative title, "Hollywood's Unmarried Husbands and Wives," it had studio chiefs shaking in their boots over a possible moral backlash from conservative fans.[21] In addition to Gable and Lombard, the other targeted couples were Charlie Chaplin and Paulette Goddard (another front-runner for the role of Scarlet), Robert Taylor and Barbara Stanwyck, and George Raft and Virginia Pine. Gable and Lombard were the first of these duos to blink, that is, making arrangements for getting married, starting with his divorce from Langham. By January 1939 Langham was in Las Vegas to begin divorce proceed-ings, Clark had finally started shooting *Gone with the Wind*, and Lombard and half of Hollywood had lost the part of Scarlet to British actress Vivien Leigh.

On 5 March 1939 Gable's divorce from Langham became official. Lombard and Gable were married on 29 March dur-ing his first break in shooting for *Gone with the Wind*. In order to avoid a media circus, the couple eloped to a getaway ceremony in the wilds of Kingman, Arizona, approximately three hundred miles by car from Hollywood. The location was the brainstorm of Otto Winkler, Gable's friend and personal MGM public relations man.

The Lombard-Gable wedding took place in Kingman's

Methodist Episcopal Chapel. In addition to Rev. Kenneth Engle and his wife, the other witnesses were Winkler and Engle's neighbor, local high school principal Howard Cate. Gable wore a blue serge business suit, and Lombard, true to her preference for black and gray, wore a gray flannel suit. Cate said the couple did not act like sophisticated screen stars, but were rather "quite lovey-dovey."[22] After their late afternoon ceremony, the couple called Lombard's mother, with Gable talking first, "Hello, Mom, this is your new son-in-law."[23] Then Lombard requested that Bessie Peters and whomever she could round up should meet them at the actress's Bel-Air home late that night.

Amusingly, print coverage of the marriage included a smoke screen that the newlyweds "would motor on to Boulder City, Nev. and spend tomorrow at Boulder Dam."[24] But as their call to Bessie clearly indicated, they had no intention of going anywhere but home. (Speaking of "creative" commentary from the couple, when they applied for their marriage license shortly before the ceremony, Lombard shaved a year off her age, making herself twenty-nine.) After calling Bessie, the couple and Winkler immediately returned by car to Los Angeles, with the men sharing driving duties over the ten-hour trip. Reaching Lombard's Bel-Air home after 2:00 A.M., there was a short celebration with the waiting Bessie, Stuart Peters, and Madalynne Fields. The exhausted newlyweds then slept separately that evening, delaying their "wedding night" until they were both rested and alone.

Moreover, MGM had scheduled a press conference for 30 March. Lombard's only regret was forgetting to honor a promise to give the wedding scoop to gossip columnist Louella Parsons. By the time Lombard remembered her promise, she was unable to locate the journalist by phone.

The Gable-Lombard union did not come cheap. Gable's divorce cost nearly $300,000, though he later enjoyed embellishing that number to $500,000. A line of dialogue from Gable's latest movie, *Idiots Delight*, seemed to satirize this sizable settlement. His character buys love interest Norma Shearer a seventy-five-cent gift and informs her, "That's the most expensive present I ever bought a dame." It cracked Lombard up each time she heard it, and she frequently found ways to needle her new husband with the line.

While the divorce settlement did not financially break Gable, as was often rumored, it did severely crimp his cash flow, as well as divesting him of all his valuable possessions save his cherished gun collection. Gable's financial setback affected how the couple paid for their dream home. The house in question was a modest two-story structure built in a New England–farmhouse style. Located on twenty acres of land in the San Fernando Valley, the home was euphemistically referred to as a "ranch." Given Gable's lack of ready cash, Lombard paid the $50,000 for the property. There was a certain irony to this, given that Gable's two earlier marriages had been to well-off women who initially had covered the bills while he was establishing himself in the movies.

WES D. GEHRING

The famous 1939 photo which often accompanied the announcement of Lombard and Gable's marriage.

The previous owner of the small ranch was director Raoul Walsh, who had used the relatively remote property (about a thirty-minute drive from MGM) as a weekend retreat. Gable and Lombard were longtime friends of Walsh, with Gable having been after the director to sell the ranch for some time. Walsh finally caved in as either a concession to the new couple or as a response to Lombard's willingness to meet his asking price in cash. The actress, who had recently been patriotically saluted by the press for her pride in paying 85 percent of her income in taxes, decided that remodeling costs for their dream home necessitated her going back to work, and she signed on for the melodramatic love triangle *In Name Only* (1939). At $150,000 a picture, Lombard remained one of Hollywood's highest-paid performers.

For *In Name Only*, Lombard played a commercial artist in love with a married man (Cary Grant) whose manipulative wife (Kay Francis) will not give him a divorce. The story also bore more than a passing resemblance to events in the actress's personal life, though one should hasten to add that Gable's most recent ex-wife was never deceitful but rather a hardball businesswoman about their divorce settlement. As with *Made for Each Other*, both Lombard and the picture garnered critical hosannas. *Variety*, calling *In Name Only* "one of the best pictures of the year," went on to add, "Grant and Miss Lombard emerge highly impressive. . . . Lombard is almost entirely on the romantic drama side, turning in a fine performance."[25] The *New York Times* observed, "Miss

WES D. GEHRING

A romantic summer day from In Name Only
(1939, with Cary Grant).

Lombard plays her poignant role with all the fragile intensity and contained passion that have lifted her to dramatic eminence."[26] The *New York Herald Tribune* said that the story creates "terrific mental strain for her [Lombard's character] and it is handsomely indicated in Miss Lombard's acting."[27]

Unfortunately, the only downside to the critically acclaimed *In Name Only*, as well as *Made for Each Other*, was that their box-office returns were soft, showing a profit but not commensurate with the glowing nature of the reviews. Although an explanation for this sort of thing is hardly an exact science (otherwise box-office hits could be routinely produced), the general consensus was that the public preferred Lombard in comedies. For example, *New York Sun* critic Eileen Creelman, though praising both the picture and the players, could not resist a parting caveat of criticism, "Miss Lombard, far more effective in rollicking comedy, enjoys only a few laughs here."[28] It was a sentiment viewers seemed to share.

With an assist from Lombard's salary for *In Name Only*, the remodeling of Walsh's former house went well into the summer, almost paralleling the January to July 1939 shooting schedule for *Gone with the Wind*. Lombard, long a fan of Laurel and Hardy, might have taken a home makeover cue from Stan Laurel. The comedian, in an effort to discourage overnight guests, had the second floor of his home converted into one large bedroom suite. Sharing the same philosophy as Laurel when it came to visitors, Lombard and Gable had the original three-bedroom second floor redesigned as separate his and her bedroom suites.

Gable's area was in masculine shades of brown and beige, with generous decorative use of wood and leather. The bedroom itself included a small bar and built-in bookcases. His bed was huge, with a large headboard of brown leather. The adjoining study included an antique desk from *Gone with the Wind*, a peace offering from Selznick. Gable, who had a cleanliness fetish after a young adulthood spent in grimy oil

ALLEN COUNTY–FORT WAYNE HISTORICAL SOCIETY

The actress "herding" geese on the Lombard-Gable "ranch."

fields, requested a beige marble bathroom whose only limi-
tation was the absence of a tub; he was strictly a shower man.
In contrast, Lombard's suite was done in white and blue and
showcased, as one Gable biographer phrased it, "the only
'Hollywood' rooms in the house."[29] The décor included crys-
tal chandeliers, white fur rugs, and a mirrored theater-style
dressing room. Her bathroom was of white marble and
accented an elaborate tub. Besides being the sole
"Hollywood rooms," one might have added they were the
lone feminine retreat, too. Of course, Lombard's description
of the bathroom was a bit earthier. She called it "the most elegant shithouse in the San Fernando Valley."[30]

Consistent with the New England–farmhouse exterior,
the signature room on the main floor was an elegant Early
American wood-paneled dining room with braided rag rugs, a
bar on one end, and a fireplace on the other. Complimenting
the masculine eating area was a gun room where Gable
housed his extensive collection of weaponry. The living room
was a shared space, supporting both Gable's preference for
minimalist furnishings of a casually contemporary style, as
well as Lombard's antique tables and a cabinet for her china
collection. The room was also peppered with vases (Lombard
loved flower arrangements) and large ashtrays, as both were
heavy smokers. For an added masculine touch, chairs and
davenports on the first floor were oversized. (The couple
employed three servants—a cook, a maid, and a butler-valet.)

How did the couple spend their time out of the lime-

Lombard and Gable as a farming couple.

light? Gable removed Lombard from that crazy entourage that often surrounded the actress earlier in her career. There were now smaller dinner parties, versus the rental of whole amusement parks. Though this was more Gable's style,

Lombard was also attempting to foster a serious image to match her move to dramatic roles. The couple played at being "gentleman farmers," too. Gable occasionally plowed with a tractor, and Lombard cared for a large menagerie. Call it her Hoosier connection or being a midwesterner at heart, but the actress had kept chickens and ducks even before she and Gable moved to the ranch. While the couple never approached the rustic life that some press coverage suggested, such as the article titled, "Carole Lombard Assuming Role of Farmer's Wife and She Rustles Eggs for Gable," they enjoyed their country getaway.[31] Moreover, many of Gable's outdoor interests had long been Lombard habits, such as horseback riding and tennis. When time would not permit hunting and fishing excursions, Lombard joined Gable in skeet shooting. The always athletic actress also found she enjoyed taking in an assortment of sporting events with her husband, from professional boxing to college football.

During the late summer and early fall of 1939, Gable and Lombard, both between films, enjoyed an idyllic honeymoon-like existence on their ranch. But by October there were film assignments to fulfill. Gable started shooting *Strange Cargo* (1940) with Joan Crawford, and Lombard began working on *Vigil in the Night* (1940) with Brian Aherne. Though diverse stories—Gable as an escaped convict and Lombard as a dedicated nurse—both were compelling dramas that were darker than what one expected of either performer.

The movie event of the year, however, was the 15

December Atlanta premiere of *Gone with the Wind*. Hailed in the South as the biggest thing since the Civil War, a circus atmosphere developed as media and fans descended upon the city. Atlanta swelled to four times its normal size as 750,000 visitors pushed the premiere population to a million people, everyone hoping to spot Gable, Lombard, and other celebrities. Not surprisingly, there were 40,000 requests for tickets to the gala opening, whereas the Grand Theatre only held 2,000.[32] Lombard had to prod Gable to attend the opening. His excuses included everything from his standard claim of uneasiness in crowds to a perceived slight to Victor Fleming, the director of *Gone with the Wind*. He was Gable's favorite director and had replaced George Cukor at the start of the production, presumably at the request of the actor. Lombard was instrumental in ironing everything out, and the Atlanta premiere was a great public success, although Gable and Selznick continued to feud in private. (Fleming used the 12 December death of his friend and mentor Douglas Fairbanks Sr. as an excuse to miss the premiere.)

Ironically, given Gable's policy of avoiding public appearances, the newsreel footage of the event depicts a handsome and assured Gable giving a brief but seemingly heartfelt tribute to the author of *Gone with the Wind*: "Ladies and gentlemen, tonight I am here just as a spectator. I want to see *Gone with the Wind* the same as you do. This is Margaret Mitchell's night, and the people of Atlanta's night. Allow me, please, to see *Gone with the Wind* as a spectator." Lombard, who

Lombard and Gable with David Selznick during the
Gone with the Wind *festivities in Atlanta.*

enjoyed coaching her husband (she had worked with him on
his comic dance number in *Idiot's Delight*), had encouraged
Gable to have something in mind in case such a situation
occurred.

Of course, the film became the biggest commercial hit of
all time. In 1939 the typical price of a film ticket was just
under a quarter. But *Gone with the Wind* rated a matinee
price of 75 cents, which escalated to more than a dollar a ticket in the evening. Although its box-office totals have been
eclipsed, largely due to ever escalating ticket prices, if a

movie's commercial success was simply based upon the number of tickets sold, the general consensus is that *Gone with the Wind* would still be number one. To Lombard's eternal credit, she not only played cheerleader to her husband's performance but was also an early fan of Vivien Leigh. The December 1939 gala could not have ended the decade on a higher note for America's favorite film couple. Sadly, this fairy-tale existence was fast approaching midnight.

10

Turning the Tables on Hitchcock
and Other Final Adventures

Lombard and Gable were anxious to have a baby.
And following the late 1939 release of Gone with the Wind,
there were recurrent stories in the newspapers that they were
expecting "a little Rhett Butler or possibly a Rhetta."[1]

CAROLE LOMBARD'S ONLY GOAL FOR 1940 WAS TO GET PREG-
nant, but rumors about her condition started surfacing soon
after her marriage to Clark Gable. Indeed, many commenta-
tors were convinced that her August 1939 hospitalization for
an appendectomy had really been a smoke screen for a mis-
carriage. The couple fueled the attention by their outspoken
desire to start a family. Lombard was so serious about the
subject that she told friends motherhood constituted grounds
for retiring from the screen. This said a lot about the
Lombard-Gable marriage, given that threats to her career
caused sparks to fly in her relationships with both William
Powell and Russ Columbo.

Still, Lombard had not given up hope of winning an
Academy Award. *Vigil in the Night* was released in early
1940, and the actress was convinced this was the one that
might win her the coveted Oscar. (Missing out earlier on an
Oscar for the 1936 *Godfrey* had so upset Lombard that

Gable had offered to give her his Oscar for *It Happened One Night*, complete to having it reengraved with her name.) Though *Vigil* was Lombard's third straight dramatic role, this hospital melodrama was by far the most somber, and it generated mixed reviews. Thus, while the *New York World-Telegram* titled its review, "'Vigil in the Night' Is Enormously Fascinating," *Variety* observed, "'Vigil' . . . is too sombre and depressing in dramatic content for general audiences."[2] Despite the critical reservations about the film, Lombard's reviews were consistently solid. For example, the *New York Post* ultimately recommended the movie due to Lombard's "excellent and grave performance as a nurse."[3] As with her previous picture, *In Name Only* (1939), however, praise was often coupled with comments directed at preferring Lombard the comedienne. The *New York Sun*'s Eileen Creelman liked *Vigil* but added, "Miss Lombard is so delightful in comedy that it seems a pity to coop her up in drama."[4]

Though *Vigil* is still considered one of the most realistic hospital movies ever made, *Variety*'s assertion that it was "too sombre" for "general audiences" unfortunately proved to be true. Box-office returns were next to nothing. Here was more apparent evidence that the movie-going public would support Lombard only in comedy. Interestingly, *Vigil*'s director George Stevens was also attempting to stretch himself beyond a comedy base. Starting out as a cameraman on Laurel and Hardy short subjects for Leo McCarey, Stevens moved to feature films in the 1930s, scoring an assortment of

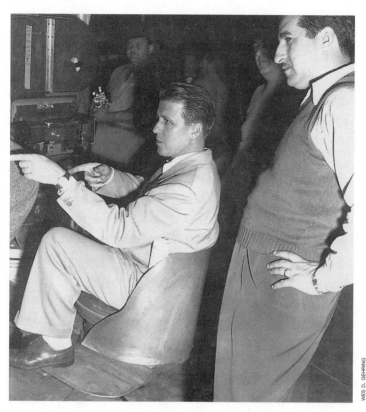

Director George Stevens (seated) at work.

hits in various comedy genres: the personality comedian venue (*Kentucky Kernels*, 1934), romantic comedy (*Alice Adams*, 1935), musical comedy (*Swing Time*, 1936), screwball comedy (*Vivacious Lady*, 1938), and others. Consequently, Lombard was attracted to working with Stevens both because she admired his earlier films and because his interest in trying straight drama matched her own desire to push herself.

Ironically, Lombard's and Stevens's disappointment over the poor commercial response to *Vigil* paralleled Gable's frustration over not winning a much-deserved Oscar for his performance in *Gone with the Wind*. The 29 February 1940 Academy Award ceremony found everyone's favorite being upset by Robert Donat for his role in *Goodbye, Mr. Chips*. As with Lombard's loss in the 1936 competition, MGM politics probably made the difference. Louis B. Mayer allegedly orchestrated behind-the-scenes voting for Donat to boost disappointing box-office returns for *Goodbye, Mr. Chips*. In contrast, *Gone with the Wind* was such a runaway smash that Mayer believed a statuette for Gable would not matter at the box office. Clark was so upset that he gave away his *It Happened One Night* (1934) Oscar to the child of a Lombard friend.

Vigil's poor commercial reception was a wake-up call for Lombard to return to comedy. When an appropriate property was not to be found, however, she was tempted yet again by a strong dramatic script that would allow her to work with two artists she admired—director Garson Kanin and Oscar-winning actor Charles Laughton. The film was *They Knew What They Wanted* (1940), from Sidney Howard's 1925 Pulitzer prize–winning play. Laughton plays an Italian winemaker in California's Napa Valley, with Lombard as a discouraged waitress who becomes his mail-order bride.

The shoot tended to be stressful, however, with Laughton attempting to dominate both Kanin and costar Lombard, who had been more of a supporting player the last time they were teamed (*White Woman*, 1933). To the general public the movie seemed like a classic collaboration of artistic types, especially after *Life* magazine published a high-profile article and photo spread on the film in late September 1940.[5] Happily for Lombard and all concerned, the picture opened to rave reviews and respectable box-office receipts. *Variety* credited the film with being "beautifully acted, [and] excellently directed," adding "it is Miss Lombard's picture and perhaps the best dramatic bit she has done."[6] The *New York Herald Tribune*'s praise for the actress also managed to suggest the moving metamorphosis her character undergoes: "Lombard is extraordinarily fine as the errant hash-slinger who starts out to marry the . . . [winemaker] for his money but is overwhelmed by his great and good love for her."[7] The *New York Journal American* equated Lombard's work in the drama with her celebrated earlier screwball roles. "Already having proven that she can take serious roles in her stride as effectively as she did crackbrained comedy parts of a few seasons back," the review stated, "Miss Lombard here establishes herself definitely as an excellent dramatic actress."[8] Such kudos allowed Lombard an honorable exit from her four-film excursion into straight drama. Although she had slowed down her movie career, she had definitely decided it was time to return to comedy.

During 1940 Gable and Lombard managed to spend a great deal of time together. Gable accompanied Lombard on location to Napa Valley during the *They Knew What They Wanted* shoot, and their ongoing relationship continued to impress Hollywood. Though only starting their second year of marriage, they had been a couple almost five years, which was five years longer than most filmland oddsmakers gave them in 1936. Gable friend and actor David Niven credited Lombard's "blonde good looks, a sense of humor, lovely wild bursts of laughter, his own brand of down-to-earthness, and . . . his love of wild country" as the basis for Gable's continued captivation.[9]

What continued to draw Lombard to Gable? Initially, as suggested in Warren G. Harris's joint biography of the couple, probably "one of his main attractions for her was the fact that he was Clark Gable."[10] Lombard was ever the competitor, and capturing the heart of the world's most popular film star was a great coup. This admittedly shallow catalyst gradually evolved into something much deeper, and she found his fatalistically unassuming personality (to the point of almost being shy) especially endearing. Indeed, James Thurber fan Lombard "had a theory that Clark's interest in acting was an expression of a Walter Mitty in him no one else seemed to sense."[11] Beyond that, she was genuinely moved by his efforts to build both a relationship and a home—two things he had not experienced before in his life.

The couple's mutual-admiration society only hit bumpy terrain when Gable occasionally succumbed to the sexual advances from an army of female fans. The situation was not without a certain irony given that such casual sex had once been a part of her life, too. But Lombard actually was more concerned by the movie stars who acted like shop girls around her husband, from the veteran merry widow Norma Shearer to newcomer Hedy Lamarr. After being immersed in Lombard material for years, however, it is fair to say that the extent of Gable's unfaithfulness has been *greatly* exaggerated. Their marriage was a work in progress, but is that not a valid statement about most relationships? Their modest ranch, what the press enjoyed punning as "the house of two Gables," was a genuinely happy home where Hollywood's star couple could unwind, Gable with his glass of Scotch and Lombard with her Coca-Cola.

At the end of a casually carefree summer for the couple, Lombard came across a comedy script she wanted to do. If not quite a screwball comedy, the story was a romantic comedy first cousin. Titled *Mr. and Mrs. Smith*, it was about a wealthy young couple who, through a residency quirk, find they are not legally married. When the husband does not act quickly enough to redress this problem, finding this unmarried relationship with his wife more provocatively titillating, the wife is insulted and throws him out. Naturally, this necessitates a whole new comic courtship, no easy matter when the wife declares herself a free agent and starts dating.

Lombard had been plowing through a great deal of scripts (she was a voracious reader of everything, while Gable concentrated on murder mysteries), but the *Mr. and Mrs. Smith* property—in spite of its slight story—was the best thing she had seen in some time. RKO did not have a director for the project, and Lombard, the quasi-producer, took it upon herself to find the right person for the job. The director she had in mind was the tenant of her former Bel-Air house, a British filmmaker by the name of Alfred Hitchcock.

Gable and Lombard had initially met Hitchcock through their ties with David O. Selznick, who had brought Hitchcock to the United States for *Rebecca* (1940). Lombard completely charmed the English director and was able to arrange for Selznick to loan Hitchcock to RKO. That the celebrated "master of suspense" should direct Lombard's romantic comedy has, both then and now, been treated as an aberration in Hitchcock's career. Yet, this is a surprisingly shallow take on the British director, as any student of Hitchcock knows comedy is never far from the surface in his films. In fact, his classic *39 Steps* (1935) is essentially an English screwball comedy mystery, with Robert Donat and Madeleine Carroll trading romantic banter with all the zest of any of their American counterparts in this genre. Moreover, screwball comedy of the period was often sprinkled with murder, such as Lombard's *The Princess Comes Across* (1936). Hitchcock needed little persuading from Lombard to accept the assignment.

While *Mr. and Mrs. Smith* was strictly a romantic comedy, Lombard had once again demonstrated her awareness of another artist's capabilities. She had been a longtime fan of Hitchcock's English films. Paradoxically, the only thing sinister, à la his suspense image, to come out of Lombard's relationship with the director was a morbid but comic personal incident that preceded her work with Hitchcock. Shortly before the Gables met the Hitchcocks, Gable gave Lombard a shrunken head, part of an ongoing tradition of gag gifts stretching back to the dilapidated Model-T Ford that had sparked their relationship.

This time, however, Gable had misread his wife, who was not amused, but ever the quick wit responded that it reminded her too much of George Raft. The events that followed, however, were amusing. Lombard pitched the gag gift out the window of their car on the way to a party but became worried that if the shrunken head were found it would somehow get the couple in trouble. Consequently, on the way home Lombard insisted they stop and search for the thing. As luck would have it, their flashlight attracted some patrolling policemen. Initially incredulous at meeting two Hollywood stars searching for a shrunken head, they ultimately responded like the patiently accommodating cops of a Laurel and Hardy movie and joined in the search.

Sometime later that evening the head was found and buried. Flash forward to the Hollywood arrival of the Hitchcocks and Lombard becoming their landlady. Following a small dinner party Hitchcock's wife, Alma, corners Lombard for advice. Telling the actress she admires the affectionately close relationship Lombard has with Gable, Alma asks for suggestions as to why her marriage has grown chilly since arriving in California. Though initially without a clue, the superstitious Lombard (a legacy from her numerology mother), eventually remembered the buried head that she had planted in the yard of the Bel-Air house. Needless to say, Lombard felt a need to exhume the head. History has neither recorded the final resting place of this most bizarre of the Gable-Lombard gag gifts, nor has it documented its impact on the Hitchcock marriage. Thankfully, the director's collaboration with Lombard was a critical and commercial hit.

Though later Lombard biographers have sometimes suggested reviews were only lukewarm, or that Hitchcock was merely slumming in a romantic comedy, a survey of the film's 1941 notices reveals a different story. For example, the *New York World-Telegram* observed, "Portly Alfred Hitchcock abandons melodrama, but not entertainment, in the frisky, scampish, gleeful comedy called Mr. and Mrs. Smith."[12] *Variety* said, "Hitchcock catches all of the laugh values from the above par script of Norman Krasna."[13] Crediting Hitchcock with the ability to stage scenes "as bright as new-minted coins," the *New York Herald Tribune* went on to pay him the ultimate compliment: "For an Englishman, Hitchcock has evidenced a keen perception of how an American couple thinks and acts."[14] Along similar lines, the *New York Post* likened Hitchcock to European Ernst Lubitsch yet in "an American farce, gay and witty and sophisticated."[15] Critic William Boehnel even went so far as to put a tongue-in-cheek curse on any reviewer questioning Hitchcock's move to pure comedy: "I understand some Hollywoodites don't like it—feel that Hitch should stick to mysteries. A plague on them!"[16]

The praise, of course, was not limited to the rotund Englishman. Lombard also garnered excellent notices as well. The *New York Times* said, "To spin this off-center comedy, one needs actors who can catch a jest on the wing. Mr. Hitchcock has them. . . . Lombard caromes through the role of Mrs. Smith as if she hadn't a brain in her head, which is what she is supposed to do."[17] The *New York Daily News* celebrated both Lombard and Hitchcock's knowing ability to draw upon their silent-film roots, noting "As most of the comedy is engendered by the facial expressions . . . [Lombard and Robert Montgomery] prove themselves adept at pantomime."[18]

Lombard not only was back as a comic actress, but she was also resurfacing as a screwball presence. Hitchcock was famous, or infamous, for the statement, "Actors should be treated as cattle." So when the director appeared for the first day of shooting, he found a small corral holding three calves with accompanying name tags for each of the stars, Lombard, Montgomery, and Gene Raymond. When it came time to shoot Hitchcock's signature cameo appearance (the also superstitious director did a guest spot for luck in each of his movies), Lombard directed the Englishman. Given both Hitchcock's statement about actors and his often demanding style, Lombard relished this opportunity for comedy pay-back, or as a contemporary article proclaimed, "Carole Lombard Gets Revenge by Directing Alfred Hitchcock."[19] The scene had Hitchcock being mistaken for a panhandler and Montgomery giving him a dime. Lombard was relentless in her direction of Hitchcock: "Try again. Now Alfie, when he gives you that dime, I want you to turn around here and pout. And when you walk down the street be subtle. I want you in a pensive mood, Alfie. [Hitchcock tries to follow Lombard's direction.] I don't like it. Stop your mumbling. [He protests.] I'd like it a little clearer. This is for an American audience."[20]

While stunts such as directing Hitchcock generated a great deal of press, Lombard was just as active with her private pranks. *Mr. and Mrs. Smith* was filmed during the height of the 1940 presidential election. Democrat Franklin D. Roosevelt broke precedent by winning a third term against GOP challenger Wendell Willkie. Lombard was a longtime Roosevelt supporter. Her costar, Montgomery, was heavily involved with Willkie's California campaign, and Lombard anonymously plastered Roosevelt bumper stickers on Montgomery's car on an almost daily basis. This might also have been comedy payback for Montgomery's suggestion that Lombard should support fellow Hoosier Willkie.

Shortly after the completion of *Mr. and Mrs. Smith*, Lombard and Gable traveled to Baltimore's Johns Hopkins Medical Center. The official explanation for the trip at the time was for treatment of a shoulder injury Gable had sustained during an early 1930s riding accident, although in later years the problem was blamed upon an accident during the filming of *San Francisco* (1936). The visit appears to have been a smoke screen to allow Lombard to check into the hospital's noted gynecology department to determine why she had not conceived. Make no mistake, the couple had been trying. A Gable-Lombard friend later shared, "They tried every position known to humans. They would have done it hanging out a window if somebody said you got pregnant that way."[21] The tests proved nonconclusive, though Lombard was advised to go easy on physical activity. She had already cut back on her filmmaking, so this new directive necessitated either less ambitious hunting and fishing trips with Gable, or her not going along at all.

Counseling such as this, however, implied that the problem was with Lombard, which she frequently believed was the case. But this was not a universal verdict. Lombard's closest friend and former private secretary, Madalynne Fields, thought such thinking was a facade to protect the macho image of America's favorite leading man. Although a definitive answer will probably never be known, history suggests that Fields was wrong. Gable had fathered a child with Loretta Young, though both he and the American public did not know about it at the time. (Young became pregnant when she costarred with Gable in 1935's *The Call of the Wild*. The incident was hushed up, and the actress later quietly adopted her own daughter.) Moreover, Gable and his fourth wife,

Kathleen Williams, also had a child, though sadly, John Clark Gable was born a few months *after* the actor's death on 16 November 1960.

Lombard and Gable's East Coast trip had an entertainingly patriotic detour in Washington, D.C. While visiting the capital for the standard sightseeing stops, President Roosevelt invited the couple to the White House, where they were part of a select audience for one of Roosevelt's famous Fireside Chats (30 December 1940). In these chats the president addressed the nation from the Oval Office via a national radio hookup. These talks were so popular that film theaters often stopped screenings and piped in Roosevelt's broadcast to attract customers. This particular Fireside Chat keyed upon the approaching clouds of war. The Gables were favorably impressed, especially Lombard, the strong Democrat. After the president's speech, the couple met privately with the Roosevelts. The topic of their half-hour audience was strictly about the movies, of which Franklin Roosevelt was a big fan.

With having a baby still her top priority, Lombard took much of 1941 off. However, Lombard realized that as much as she wanted a family, she could never entirely give up films. Journalist Gladys Hall might have best captured the actress's passion for the movies in a casual comment made in a late-1938 article: Lombard "studies a script until the ink is absorbed right off the page."[22] A reference to reading scripts was particularly apt for Lombard in 1941, as this was her only connection to the movies for much of the year. She not only read potential scripts for herself but also ones MGM sent home with Gable. Always a great judge of material, she was particularly taken with the script *Woman of the Year*, which would eventually become the first of many memorable Spencer Tracy-Katharine Hepburn films. Lombard thought it might make an excellent joint venture for her and Gable, but soon discovered that Hepburn held the rights to the script. Although she encouraged her husband to consider the role, he believed it was too much a woman's picture. Plus, he had no interest in costarring with Hepburn. Nevertheless, the role of a sportswriter who tames an ice-goddess would have fit Gable like a glove.

Paradoxically, when the couple saw a sneak preview of the picture, Gable felt even more certain he could not have played the role, while Lombard was convinced her husband would have stolen the show. Part of Gable's feeling of inferiority was probably tied to his great admiration for the acting range of his friend Tracy. Ironically, while Gable was supportive of Tracy's performing skills, Tracy was frequently jealous of both Gable's charismatic good looks and greater box-office clout. As Lombard was finding out, for all Gable's acclaim he was at heart a very modest man. This was best demonstrated by his answer to a journalist's question on what his epitaph should be: "He was lucky, and he knew it." In contrast, the methodically controlling Lombard would have replied: "Luck had nothing to do with it."

With so much time on her hands in 1941, Lombard was

going a little stir-crazy. There were, however, more modest hunting and fishing trips, not to mention sporting events and small dinner parties. When home alone, if the couple were not reading, they enjoyed playing penny poker, backgammon, and the occasional odd job on their ranch. The evening meal was never early. Gable's new MGM contract had him home by six o'clock, but he liked to read the mail, unwind over a drink, and discuss the events of the day, from studio politics to the war in Europe. Lombard was also becoming something of a radio junkie, especially when it involved the programs of comedian friends such as Jack Benny or George Burns and Gracie Allen.

By the summer of 1941, Lombard's cabin fever escalated to the point that the couple, although still hoping for a baby, decided that she should consider another film project. It would most definitely be a comedy, since Lombard was resigned to the fact that this was how the public preferred her. Moreover, with the gloomy news of impending global war, the actress believed a comedy was what the public needed most. It was just a matter of finding a suitable property, which was no easy task. Lombard had always been on the lookout for material, even when motherhood had become her number one priority, but nothing had surfaced.

Help soon came from a comedy colleague. When the word filtered out into the Hollywood community that Lombard was looking for a comic film, Benny brought the black-comedy script *To Be or Not to Be* to her attention. A satire of the Nazi takeover of Poland, the story was topical but controversial, especially with the United States not yet in the war. It was the pet project of Ernst Lubitsch, Lombard's old friend at Paramount. Through the years, various contacts have been cited for bringing Lombard to the film, but Lubitsch's biographer, Scott Eyman, makes the best case for crediting Benny.[23]

Benny's campaign for Lombard was not purely an act of friendship. Because Benny was perceived as more of a radio comedian than a film star, this provocative independent project needed a "name" performer to guarantee its funding. Ultimately, Lubitsch was flattered by Lombard's interest, but he believed that her enthusiasm for the project would wane after reading the script.

To Lubitsch's surprise, Lombard was charmed by the script, which involved a husband and wife acting duo who were part of a Warsaw theatrical troupe on the eve of World War II. When the Nazi invasion occurs, this Polish company uses their art to thwart the enemy. Although Lombard's part was secondary to Benny's lead, she correctly saw *To Be or Not to Be* as an ensemble piece, with some of the most pivotal scenes actually given to relatively minor characters. Always the team player, Lombard appreciated this approach. There were other positive factors pushing her toward joining the cast as Maria Tura. First, since her early days at Paramount she had always wanted to star in a Lubitsch picture. He had supervised her *Hands Across the Table* (1935), but this time he would be directing. Second, though she was rededicating her career to comedy, *To Be or Not to Be* had a timely satirical bite. She saw this picture as her contribution to America's fight against global terrorism. Third, even though the script's black-comedy foundation was a bit unsettling to Lombard, she felt that with Lubitsch at the helm it would work. She would probably have concurred with the *Hollywood Reporter* critic who observed of Lubitsch, "The directorial hand of a man incapable of indifferent work."[24] Lombard placed Lubitsch and Charlie Chaplin a notch above the rest of Hollywood. Indeed, Chaplin's then recent critical and commercial success with another black comedy, *The Great Dictator* (1940), made her all the more anxious to sign on for this satire.

The shoot, which started in October 1941, proved to be a pleasant experience for the actress. As with *Hands Across the Table*, Lubitsch allowed Lombard to act as an unofficial producer on the film. She had been out of the movie loop nearly a year, and Lombard was overjoyed to be back. As with her assistance to insecure leading man Fred MacMurray on *Hands Across the Table*, Lombard spent a great deal of time helping Benny through his *To Be or Not to Be* role. He was a superb comedian, but very insecure about being the star of a picture by the great Lubitsch.

Lombard was so excited about the film she broke her self-imposed rule about only working when Gable had a film assignment. While Gable could handle this, he was not happy about her working with Lubitsch. Where Lombard saw an artist, her husband saw a German hedonist (Gable privately referred to him as "the horny Hun").[25] There was a certain symmetry for Lombard having Lubitsch as her final director. As with Chaplin, Lubitsch continued a silent film directing technique—acting out each part for every major performer in the movie, reminding Lombard of her Mack Sennett beginnings.

The movie was still in production on 7 December 1941 when the Japanese bombing of Pearl Harbor ultimately brought the United States into war against Japan and Germany. Now Lombard saw *To Be or Not to Be* as even more of a patriotic film. The film's black-comedy base, however, put it ahead of its time for many viewers. The most sensitive pronouncement along these lines came later from *New York Post* critic Archer Winsten. Suggesting the movie might polarize viewers, he confessed to being caught in the middle, "enjoying the show but not entirely at ease over the transitions from drama to comedy and back again."[26]

Immediately after America's declaration of war on 8 December, Lombard wrote to President Roosevelt offering both her services and Gable's in whatever capacity was needed. The president wrote back that Lombard and Gable could best serve the country by continuing to make movies.

To Be or Not to Be finished shooting just before Christmas. It had been a pleasant production for Lombard, especially her comically bantering relationship with Benny. Among other things, she enjoyed kidding his effeminate signature walk by calling him "Auntie." Generous as usual with her wrap-party gifts, she left early to join Gable at MGM, where he was hosting a studio festivity for servicemen. Gable was also the head of the Hollywood Victory Committee, the organization established shortly after Pearl Harbor to aid the war effort, from entertaining troops to selling war bonds.

Christmas was relatively austere for the Gables. Lombard normally went all out for friends and family, but this year a great deal of money was donated to the Red Cross in the name of loved ones. Gable presented his wife with diamond and ruby jewelry, while Lombard's primary present to her husband was an elegant gold cigarette case. The couple differed on how they should respond to the war effort. While Gable was willing to follow the president's suggestion to continue making movies, the jingoistic Lombard was relentless in "encouraging" the over-forty Gable to enter the armed forces. Lombard was bouncing off the walls with patriotic fervor, and a compromise of sorts was reached when Gable sent his wife to Indianapolis for the country's first World War II bond rally.

There were to have been more pictures with Lubitsch and a project with gifted writer-director Preston Sturges. These were not to be. Lombard and her mother died in a fiery plane crash on their way home from a very successful Indiana war-bond rally. Gable and a shocked nation mourned the passing of America's beloved screwball. Gable spent the rest of his life looking for another Lombard. As film historian Leonard Maltin movingly suggested, so would the rest of the nation, but there is no replacing an original.[27]

WES D. GEHRING

*A night on the town for the couple that was Hollywood royalty
to Americans during the Great Depression—
Lombard and Gable, circa 1939.*

Lombard's Legacy

"Hey Pappy, you better get in this man's army!"
CAROLE LOMBARD'S LAST TELEGRAM TO CLARK GABLE

THERE IS NO SET PATTERN AS TO HOW AN AUDIENCE WILL respond to a film released after the death of its star. For example, when Will Rogers, America's favorite all-around entertainer of the Great Depression, died in a 1935 plane crash, his *Steamboat 'Round the Bend* went on to be a huge box-office smash. After the death of Jean Harlow, her *Saratoga* (1937, costarring Gable) was also a commercial hit. But when Gable died before the release of *The Misfits* (1961, costarring Marilyn Monroe), the grosses were weak, despite generally positive reviews.

Lombard's last picture, *To Be or Not to Be*, which opened the month after her January 1942 death, went the way of *The Misfits*. Its less-than-stellar performance at the box office, however, cannot simply be blamed upon depressed fans staying away from the film. A greater factor was no doubt the movie's dark content. *New York Times* critic Bosley Crowther was scathing in his attack on the picture: "To say it is callous and macabre is understating the case."[1] Ironically, the type of dialogue that most offended Crowther is now routinely quoted as an entertainingly classic example of the film's dark comedy writing. Sig Rumann's comic Nazi criticizes Jack Benny's in-film *Hamlet* performance by observing, "What he did to Shakespeare we are doing now to Poland."

Despite such reservations by the influential Crowther, one should hasten to add that with a few exceptions the film was both a major critical success and a posthumous triumph for Lombard. *New York Mirror* reviewer Lee Mortimer summed it up best: "Not even Carole Lombard could have asked for a finer or more fitting farewell to a memorable career than the smooth and brilliant performance she leaves with us in this . . . delightful comedy-drama."[2] *Newsweek* said, "Lombard has never been better. . . . Her Maria Tura is an attractive, intelligently humorous characterization that is all too rare on the screen and will be rarer from now on."[3] Added the *New York World-Telegram*, "Her charm, her warmth, her felicity, her light-heartedness are here memorialized in an extraordinarily audacious film."[4]

It is important to add that *To Be or Not to Be* was not scoring mere pity points with the nation's critics. More than sixty years after the movie's release, the American Film Institute selected it as one of the one hundred funniest movies ever made, ranking the picture at number forty-nine. Given that only one other Lombard film made the AFI list (1936's *My Man Godfrey*, at number forty-four), this documents that the actress died at a high point in her career.

WES D. GEHRING

Jack Benny decked out as Hamlet in a scene from To Be or Not to Be
(1942, with a seated Lombard and Maude Edurne.)

Paradoxically, this parallels the only comfort Lombard was
able to glean from the shocking deaths of Harlow and Russ
Columbo, they were at the height of their fame and artistry.
Now it applied to Lombard, too.

The box office for *To Be or Not to Be* was also hurt by the
limited theater access of the film's distributor, United Artists.
Indeed, Lombard's earlier films for independent producer
David O. Selznick, including *Nothing Sacred* (1937) and *Made*

for Each Other (1939), had also been hurt commercially by the United Artists's weak distribution system. One final factor that might have affected the box office of *To Be or Not to Be* involved what was perceived at the time as macabre parallels between the movie and Lombard's death in a plane crash. That is, Lombard's character is romantically involved with a flyer (Robert Stack), and the film concludes with an air escape from Nazi-occupied Warsaw. These dark coincidences produced negative word of mouth among 1942 movie patrons.[5]

The film's modern status as a classic is yet another example of Lombard's ability to be ahead of her time. *To Be or Not to Be*'s pioneering standing as a black comedy is not the only thing that modern viewers appreciate. Today the movie's screwball component, driven by Lombard's continued cuckolding of antiheroic Benny, is also fully recognized. And for that reason, it now seems all the more fitting a finale for Lombard.

The AFI notwithstanding, *To Be or Not to Be* and *My Man Godfrey* represent only part of Lombard's movie legacy. She has three other bona fide classics in her filmography: the pioneer screwball comedy *Twentieth Century* (1934), the Ernst Lubitsch produced combination of romantic and screwball comedy *Hands Across the Table* (1935), and the darkly comic screwball outing *Nothing Sacred* (1937). One might also exercise some revisionist criticism and elevate Lombard's often inspired *The Princess Comes Across* (1936) to pantheon status. Thus, Lombard was averaging a memorable movie a year before she slowed down her career in the late 1930s. This says nothing of countless near great cinema outings, from her teaming with Gable in the charming romantic drama *No Man of Her Own* (1932), to the poignant comedy-melodrama *Made for Each Other* (1939) with Jimmy Stewart.

Lombard also proved to be an actress with an impressive genre range, from the now cult classic horror film *Supernatural* (1933) to the melodramatic *In Name Only* (1939, with Cary Grant). Her contemporary public's preference for seeing her in screwball comedy, however, still holds true today. In this genre her every action is mesmerizing, and while she performed admirably in other types of films, her screwball personae defined that genre. The fact that these outings are often peppered with dark undertones, from claiming to be fatally ill in *Nothing Sacred*, to pretending to be a murderer in the underrated *True Confession* (1937), makes the films all the more timely for modern audiences.

This often zany Lombard film legacy is especially central to how she is remembered, because it is so closely identified with the real person. Even though a blurred distinction between performing and reality is a common occurrence among fans celebrating movie stars, Lombard pushed the phenomenon to a higher level in three ways. First, Lombard was known as an eccentric, from goofy parties to comically provocative observations on a litany of subjects. Second, screwball comedy is famous for its actors playing variations of their real identities. Director Howard Hawks cast Lombard in her breakthrough film, *Twentieth Century*, based upon her free-spirited private antics. Plus, Hawks directed her to be herself, an approach reinforced by Gregory LaCava in her greatest movie, *My Man Godfrey*. Third, Noel F. Busch cemented the connection between the private and public Lombard in an article for *Life* magazine with his amusing declaration: "The world's No. 1 attractive neurotic might well in her private life be as placid as a Hollywood cow at twilight. This point however cannot be proved by the character or career of Carole Lombard. Her personal behavior is certainly as kaleidoscopic as that of the characters she impersonates."[6]

This viewer identification with Lombard undoubtedly made her death at only thirty-three years old all the more difficult for the public to accept. Link this tragedy to the early troubled days of World War II, and one has a take on a Lombard legacy that now is all but forgotten—war hero. This patriotic position was further cemented at the time by the actions of her grieving husband. More than forty and with a directive from President Franklin D. Roosevelt to keep making movies, Gable opted to honor Lombard's request to join "this man's army."

After finishing the war-related and ironically labeled *Somewhere I'll Find You* (1942, which had been in production when Lombard died), Gable enlisted in the Army Air Corps. In a combination of grief and patriotism, he trained for the most dangerous and hard-to-recruit position in the air service, tail gunner on a B-17 bomber. After several bombing missions over Germany, he received the Distinguished Flying Cross and Air Medal. But maybe his greatest war distinction was having Hitler put the equivalent of a $5,000 reward out for his capture. It seems that Gable had been the dictator's favorite prewar actor, and he was most distressed that the star was now flying bombing missions over Germany.

Gable believed that Lombard would have gotten a special kick out of these Hitler stories. (The dark side of the German bounty was that Gable never wore a parachute, he was not going to be taken alive.) But the fact remains that Gable would not have had to put himself in harm's way. Many major stars younger than Gable, such as John Wayne and Bing Crosby, stayed at home to make patriotic movies. This linkage of Lombard as both a symbol of patriotism and a catalyst for her husband's own patriotism was further cemented in the public's perception by the launching of the Liberty ship *Carole Lombard* in early 1944. It was the beginning of yet another bond campaign, and Gable spoke to a christening crowd of more than 15,000. There was even a screwball footnote to the festivities, another actress associated with the genre, Indiana-reared Irene Dunne, christened the ship.

The ceremony proved to be Gable's most difficult mission of the war. He managed to get through his speech, but when Dunne broke the champagne bottle on the ship's hull, Gable began to weep openly, something he had not done at Lombard's funeral. During this apparent moment of patriotic closure Gable might have thought of the last line of

President Roosevelt's telegram of condolence: "She is and always will be a star, one we shall never forget, nor cease to be grateful to." This metaphorical "reading" of the term "star," for both patriot and movie personality, had never been more true than the launching of the Liberty ship *Carole Lombard*. For Gable and the rest of the nation, Lombard now belonged to the ages.

Lombard Filmography

March 1921	*A Perfect Crime* (approximately 50 minutes) Director/Screenplay: Allan Dwan, from the Carl Clausen story. Stars: Monte Blue, Jacqueline Logan, Stanton Heck, Hardee Kirkland, Jane Peters [Carole Lombard].
February 1925	*Dick Turpin* (72 minutes) Director: John G. Blystone. Screenplay: Charles Kenyon and Charles Darnton. Stars: Tom Mix. [Lombard's footage was cut to a group shot.]
April 1925	*Gold and the Girl* (53 minutes) Director: Edmund Mortimer. Screenplay: John Stone. Stars: Buck Jones, Elinor Fair, Bruce Gordon, Lucien Littlefield, Claude Peyton, Carol Lombard [Carol with an *e* does not occur until 1930's *Fast and Loose*].
April 1925	*Marriage in Transit* (53 minutes) Director: Roy William Neill. Screenplay: Dorothy Yost, from the Grace Livingston Hill novel. Stars: Edmund Lowe, Carol Lombard.
June 1925	*Hearts and Spurs* (52 minutes) Director: W. S. Van Dyke. Screenplay: John Stone. Stars: Buck Jones, Carol Lombard.

October 1925   *Durand of the Badlands* (62 minutes)
Director/Screenplay: Lynn Reynolds. Cast:
Buck Jones, Marion Nixon.

February 1926   *The Road to Glory* (66 minutes)
Director: Howard Hawks. Screenplay: Hawks
and L. G. Rigby. Stars: May McAvoy, Leslie
Fenton. [Lombard's car accident occurred during this production. She lost her small role but
still appears in two large group shots.]

Lombard's Mack Sennett Short Subjects:

September 1927   *Smith's Pony* (approximately 20 minutes)

December 1927   *The Girl from Everywhere* (approximately 20
minutes)

January 1928   *Run, Girl, Run* (approximately 20 minutes)
The Beach Club (approximately 20 minutes)

February 1928   *The Best Man* (approximately 20 minutes)
The Swim Princess (approximately 20 minutes)

March 1928   *The Bicycle Flirt* (approximately 20 minutes)

August 1928   *The Girl from Nowhere* (approximately 20 minutes)
His Unlucky Night (approximately 20 minutes)

September 1928   *The Campus Vamp* (approximately 20 minutes)

March 1929   *Matchmaking Mamas* (approximately 20 minutes)

❧   ❧   ❧

July 1928   *The Divine Sinner* (60 minutes)
Director: Scott Pembroke. Screenplay: Robert
Dillon. Stars: Vera Reynolds, Nigel de Brulier,
Bernard Siegel, Ernest Hilliard, Carol Lombard.

September 1928   *Power* (60 minutes)
Director: Howard Higgin. Screenplay: Tay

Garnett. Stars: William Boyd, Alan Hale,
Jacqueline Logan, Jerry Drew, Carol Lombard.

October 1928   *Me, Gangster* (70 minutes)
Director: Raoul Walsh. Screenplay: Walsh and
Charles Francis Coe, from Coe's original story.
Stars: June Collyer, Don Terry. [Lombard has a
minor part.]

October 1928   *Show Folks* (70 minutes)
Director: Paul L. Stein. Screenplay: Jack
Jungmeyer and George Dromgold. Stars: Eddie
Quillan, Lina Basquette, Carol Lombard.

December 1928   *Ned McCobb's Daughter* (71 minutes)
Director: William J. Cowen. Screenplay: Marie
Beulah Dix, from the Sidney Howard play.
Stars: Irene Rich, Theodore Roberts, Robert
Armstrong, George Baeraud, George Hearn,
Carol Lombard.

July 1929   *High Voltage* (57 minutes)
Director: Howard Higgin. Screenplay: Elliott
Clawson, with dialogue by James Gleason.
Stars: William Boyd, Carol Lombard.

September 1929   *Big News* (75 minutes)
Director: Gregory LaCava. Screenplay: Walter
De Leon, with dialogue by Frank Reicher, from
the George S. Brooks play, *For Two Cents*.
Stars: Robert Armstrong, Carol Lombard.

November 1929   *The Racketeer* (66 minutes)
Director: Howard Higgin. Screenplay: Paul
Gangelin, with dialogue by A. A. Kline. Stars:
Robert Armstrong, Carol Lombard.

April 1930   *The Arizona Kid* (83 minutes)
Director: Alfred Santell. Screenplay: Ralph Block
and Joseph Wright, from the Block story. Stars:
Warner Baxter, Mona Maris, Carol Lombard.

July 1930	*Safety in Numbers* (78 minutes) Director: Victor Schertzinger. Screenplay: Marion Dix, from the George Marion Jr. and Percy Heath story. Stars: Charles "Buddy" Rogers, Kathryn Crawford, Joseph Dunn, Carol Lombard.
November 1930	*Fast and Loose* (75 minutes) Director: Fred Newmeyer. Screenplay: Doris Anderson, with dialogue by Preston Sturges, from the David Gray and Avery Hopwood play *The Best People*. Stars: Miriam Hopkins, Carole Lombard. [Her first credit as Carole with an *e*.]
February 1931	*It Pays to Advertise* (66 minutes) Director: Frank Tuttle. Screenplay: Arthur Kober, from the Roi Cooper Megrue and Walter Hackett play. Stars: Norman Foster, Carole Lombard, Skeets Gallagher, Eugene Pallette.
March 1931	*Man of the World* (71 minutes) Director: Richard Wallace and Edward Goodman. Screenplay: Herman J. Mankiewicz. Stars: William Powell, Carole Lombard.
May 1931	*Ladies' Man* (70 minutes) Director: Lothar Mendes. Screenplay: Herman J. Mankiewicz. Stars: William Powell, Kay Francis, Carole Lombard.
June 1931	*Up Pops the Devil* (75 minutes) Director: Edward Sutherland. Screenplay: Arthur Kober and Eve Unsell, from the Albert Hackett and Frances Goodrich play. Stars: Richard Gallogher, Stuart Erwin, Carole Lombard.
June 1931	*I Take This Woman* (74 minutes) Director: Marion Gering and Slavko Vorkapich. Screenplay: Vincent Lawrence, from the Mary Roberts Rinehart novel *Lost Ecstasy*. Stars: Gary Cooper, Carole Lombard.

January 1932	*No One Man* (72 minutes) Director: Lloyd Corrigan. Screenplay: Sidney Buchman, Agnes Brand Leahy, and Percy Heath, from a novel by Rupert Hughes. Stars: Carole Lombard, Ricardo Cortez, Paul Lukas.
May 1932	*Sinners in the Sun* (70 minutes) Director: Alexander Hall. Screenplay: Vincent Lawrence, Waldemar Young, and Samuel Hoffenstein, from the Mildred Cram story "The Beachcomber." Stars: Carole Lombard, Chester Morris, Alison Skipworth, Walter Byron, Reginald Barlow, Cary Grant.
October 1932	*Virtue* (69 minutes) Director: Edward Buzzell. Screenplay: Robert Riskin, from the Ethel Hill story. Stars: Carole Lombard, Pat O'Brien, Ward Bond.
December 1932	*No More Orchids* (72 minutes) Director: Walter Lang. Screenplay: Gertrude Purcell, from the Grace Perkins story. Stars: Carole Lombard, Walter Connolly.
December 1932	*No Man of Her Own* (85 minutes) Director: Wesley Ruggles. Screenplay: Maurine Watkins and Milton Gropper, from the Edmund Goulding and Benjamin Glazer story. Stars: Clark Gable, Carole Lombard.
February 1933	*From Hell to Heaven* (70 minutes) Director: Erle C. Kenton. Screenplay: Percy Heath and Sidney Buchman, from the Lawrence Hazard story. Stars: Carole Lombard, Jack Oakie.
April 1933	*Supernatural* (64 minutes) Director: Victor Halperin. Screenplay: Harvey Thew and Brian Marlow, from the Garnett Weston story. Stars: Carole Lombard, Randolph Scott.

May 1933	*The Eagle and the Hawk* (68 minutes) Director: Stuart Walker. Screenplay: Bogart Rogers and Seton I. Miller, from the John Monk Saunders story. Stars: Fredric March, Cary Grant, Jack Oakie, Carole Lombard.
August 1933	*Brief Moment* (69 minutes) Director: David Burton. Screenplay: Brian Marlow and Edith Fitzgerald, from the S. N. Behrman play. Stars: Carole Lombard, Gene Raymond.
November 1933	*White Woman* (69 minutes) Director: Stuart Walker. Screenplay: Samuel Hoffenstein and Gladys Lehman, from a Norman Reilly Raine and Frank Butler story. Stars: Charles Laughton, Carole Lombard, Charles Bickford.
February 1934	*Bolero* (71 minutes) Director: Wesley Ruggles. Screenplay: Horace Jackson, from a Carey Wilson and Kubec Glasmon story. Stars: George Raft, Carole Lombard, William Frawley.
April 1934	*We're Not Dressing* (77 minutes) Director: Norman Taurog. Screenplay: Horace Jackson, Francis Martin, and George Marion Jr., from a Benjamin Glazer story adaptation of James M. Barrie's *The Admirable Crichton*. Stars: Bing Crosby, Carole Lombard, George Burns, Gracie Allen, Ethel Merman, Leon Errol, Ray Milland.
May 1934	*Twentieth Century* (91 minutes) Director: Howard Hawks. Screenplay: Ben Hecht and Charles MacArthur, from their play. Stars: John Barrymore, Carole Lombard, Walter Connolly, Roscoe Karns.

October 1934	*Now and Forever* (81 minutes) Director: Henry Hathaway. Screenplay: Vincent Lawrence and Sylvia Thalliery, from a Jack Kirkland and Melville Baker story. Stars: Gary Cooper, Carole Lombard, Shirley Temple.
October 1934	*Lady by Choice* (78 minutes) Director: David Burton. Screenplay: Jo Swerling, from a Dwight Taylor story, inspired by Damon Runyon characters. Stars: Carole Lombard, May Robson, Roger Pryor, Walter Connolly.
December 1934	*The Gay Bride* (80 minutes) Director: Jack Conway. Screenplay: Bella and Samuel Spewack, from the Charles Francis Coe play *Repeal*. Stars: Carole Lombard, Chester Morris, Zasu Pitts, Leo Carrillo, Nat Pendleton.
February 1935	*Rumba* (77 minutes) Director: Marion Gering. Screenplay: Howard J. Green, additional dialogue by Harry Ruskin and Frank Partas, from a Guy Endore and Seena Owen story. Stars: George Raft, Carole Lombard.
October 1935	*Hands Across the Table* (80 minutes) Director: Mitchell Leisen. Screenplay: Norman Krasna, Vincent Laurence, and Herbert Fields, from a Vina Delmar story. Stars: Carole Lombard, Fred MacMurray, Ralph Bellamy.
March 1936	*Love before Breakfast* (70 minutes) Director: Walter Lang. Screenplay: Herbert Fields, from Faith Baldwin's novel. Stars: Carole Lombard, Preston Foster, Janet Beecher, Cesar Romero.
May 1936	*The Princess Comes Across* (76 minutes) Director: William K. Howard. Screenplay:

Walter De Leon, Francis Martin, Frank Butler, and Don Hartman, story by Philip MacDonald from a Louis Lucien Rogger novel. Stars: Carole Lombard, Fred MacMurray, Douglas Dumbrille, Alison Skipworth, William Frawley.

September 1936   *My Man Godfrey* (95 minutes)
Director: Gregory LaCava. Screenplay: Morrie Ryskind and Eric Hatch, from Hatch's novel, with uncredited additional material by LaCava. Stars: William Powell, Carole Lombard, Alice Brady, Gail Patrick, Jean Dixon, Eugene Pallette, Alan Mowbray, Mischa Auer.

March 1937   *Swing High, Swing Low* (95 minutes)
Director: Mitchell Leisen. Screenplay: Virginia Van Upp and Oscar Hammerstein II, from the George Manker Watters and Arthur Hopkins play *Burlesque*. Stars: Carole Lombard, Fred MacMurray, Charles Butterworth, Jean Dixon.

November 1937   *Nothing Sacred* (75 minutes)
Director: William Wellman. Screenplay: Ben Hecht, from a William Street story. Stars: Carole Lombard, Fredric March, Charles Winninger, Walter Connolly.

December 1937   *True Confession* (85 minutes)
Director: Wesley Ruggles. Screenplay: Claude Binyon, from the Louis Verneuil and Georges Berr play *Mon Crime*. Stars: Carole Lombard, Fred MacMurray, John Barrymore, Una Merkel, Porter Hall, Edgar Kennedy.

April 1938   *Fools for Scandal* (81 minutes)
Director: Mervyn Le Roy. Screenplay: Herbert and Joseph Fields, additional dialogue by Irving Beecher, from a Nancy Hamilton, James Shute, and Rosemary Casey play *Return Engagement*. Stars: Carole Lombard, Fernand

Gravet, Ralph Bellamy, Allen Jenkins.

February 1939	*Made for Each Other* (93 minutes) Director: John Cromwell. Screenplay: Jo Swerling. Stars: Carole Lombard, James Stewart, Charles Coburn.
August 1939	*In Name Only* (94 minutes) Director: John Cromwell. Screenplay: Richard Sherman, from the Bessie Breuer novel *Memory of Love*. Stars: Carole Lombard, Cary Grant, Kay Francis, Charles Coburn.
February 1940	*Vigil in the Night* (96 minutes) Director: George Stevens. Screenplay: Fred Guidl, P. J. Wolfson, Rowland Leigh, from the A. J. Cronin novel. Stars: Carole Lombard, Brian Aherne, Anne Shirley.
October 1940	*They Knew What They Wanted* (96 minutes) Director: Garson Kanin. Screenplay: Robert Ardrey, from the Sidney Howard play. Stars: Carole Lombard, Charles Laughton, William Gargan, Harry Carey.
February 1941	*Mr. and Mrs. Smith* (95 minutes) Director: Alfred Hitchcock. Screenplay: Norman Krasna. Stars: Carole Lombard, Robert Montgomery, Gene Raymond, Jack Carson.
February 1942	*To Be or Not to Be* (108 minutes) Director: Ernst Lubitsch. Screenplay: Edwin Justus Mayer, from a Lubitsch and Melchior Lengyel story. Stars: Carole Lombard, Jack Benny, Robert Stack.

NOTES

Preface

1. Walker Percy, *The Moviegoer* (New York: Vintage Books, 1961).

2. Noel F. Busch, "A Loud Cheer for the Screwball Girl," *Life*, 17 October 1938, pp. 48–51, 62–64.

3. Cameron Crowe, *Conversations with Wilder* (New York: Knopf, 2001), 93.

4. Molly Haskell, *Love and Other Infectious Diseases: A Memoir* (New York: William Morrow and Co., 1990), 51.

5. Rebecca Wells, *Divine Secrets of the Ya-Ya Sisterhood* (New York: HarperCollins, 1996).

Prologue

1. "Carole Lombard Predicts Indiana Will Lead Nation in Bond Sales," *Indianapolis Star*, 16 January 1942.

2. Wes D. Gehring, *Charlie Chaplin: A Bio-Bibliography* (Westport, Conn.: Greenwood Press, 1983), 26.

3. Wes D. Gehring, *Seeing Red: The Skelton in Hollywood's Closet* (Davenport, Iowa: Robin Vincent, 2001), 54–55.

4. Cobbett Steinberg, *Reel Facts: The Movie Book of Records* (New York: Vintage Books, 1978), 404.

5. David L. Smith, "Carole Lombard: Profane Angel," *Films of the Golden Age* (summer 2001): 35.

6. Ibid.

7. "Carole Lombard Gladly Gives Government Most of

Income," *Fort Wayne News-Sentinel*, 25 August 1938.

8. "War Rally Will Have Military Fanfare—and Carole Lombard," *Indianapolis News*, 14 January 1942.

9. "Carole Lombard Predicts Indiana Will Lead Nation in Bond Sales."

10. Marcia Winn, "A Whirlwind! It Was Carole on Chicago Visit," *Chicago Tribune*, 18 January 1942.

11. Ibid.

12. David Denby, "Pauline Kael," *The New Yorker*, 17 September 2001, p. 158.

13. Pauline Kael, *Movie Love: Complete Reviews, 1988–1991* (New York: Plume, 1991), 188.

14. Frederick C. Othman, "Hollywood Recalls Carole's Pranks with Chuckle and Sigh," *Indianapolis News*, 10 January 1942.

15. Frederick C. Othman, "Two Great Sorrows Marked the Life of Carole Lombard," *Indianapolis News*, 21 January 1942.

16. Larry Swindell, *Screwball: The Life of Carole Lombard* (New York: William Morrow and Co., 1975), 296–97.

17. "Hoosiers Answer Bond Sale Call," *Indianapolis News*, 15 January 1942.

18. "CATASTROPHE: End of a Mission," *Time*, 26 January 1942, p. 17.

19. Photo caption, *Indianapolis News*, 16 January 1942.

20. Mabel Wheeler Shideler, "Carole Called Victory Girl at War Rally," *Indianapolis News*, 16 January 1942.

21. Ibid.

22. Gladys Hall, "Lombard—As She Sees Herself," *Motion Picture* (November 1938): 34–35, 66, 68.

23. "Clark Works while Carole Sells Bonds," *Indianapolis Star*, 16 January 1942.

24. Shideler, "Carole Called Victory Girl at War Rally."

25. Ibid.

26. Swindell, *Screwball*, 297.

27. Mary E. Bostwick, "Carole Lombard Has Guests at Tea Selling Defense Bonds to Each Other," *Indianapolis Star*, 16 January 1942.

28. Florence Webster Long, "Glamour Given to Bond Sale by Film Star," *Indianapolis News*, 16 January 1942.

29. Bostwick, "Carole Lombard Has Guests at Tea Selling Defense Bonds to Each Other."

30. "Carole Lombard Predicts Indiana Will Lead Nation In Bond Sales."

31. Long, "Glamour Given to Bond Sale by Film Star."

32. "Carole Told of Plans to Do Bit in War Effort," *Fort Wayne Journal-Gazette*, 18 January 1942.

33. "Carole Lombard Dies in Crash after Aiding U.S. Defense Bond Campaign," *Life*, 26 January 1942, p. 25.

34. Numbers noted in Robert D. Matzen's *Carole Lombard: A Bio-Bibliography* (Westport, Conn.: Greenwood Press, 1988), 37.

35. "'Don't Take That Plane'—Mother's Warning Plea Here," *Indianapolis News*, 17 January 1942.

36. "CATASTROPHE," 17.

37. "Carole Lombard Dies in Crash after Aiding U.S. Defense Bond Campaign," 25.

38. "Simplicity to Mark Lombard Funeral Rites," *Fort Wayne News-Sentinel*, 20 January 1942.

39. The quotes from Walter Pidgeon, Errol Flynn, and James Cagney were taken from "Friend Is Gone: A Hush Falls on Hollywood," *Chicago Tribune*, 18 January 1942.

40. "Eastern Press Is Sympathetic," *Indianapolis News*, 19 January 1942.

41. Ibid.

42. "Tragedy Saddens Filmland, for Carole Was a Friend of Everyone," *Indianapolis News*, 17 January 1942.

Chapter 1

1. Robert Baral, "Blonde Beauty Grows Up," *Photoplay* (May 1939): 34.

2. James Thurber, *My Life and Hard Times* (1933; reprint, New York: Bantam Books, 1947), 50.

3. Larry Swindell, *Screwball: The Life of Carole Lombard* (New York: William Morrow and Co., 1975), 26.

4. "Carole Lombard Tells: 'How I Live by a Man's Code,'" *Photoplay* (June 1937): 13.

5. Frederick Russell, "The Life Story of Carole Lombard," part one, *Film Pictorial* (27 June 1936): 11.

6. See Peter Bogdanovich, *Who the Devil Made It* (New York: Ballantine Books, 1997), 83.

7. Swindell, *Screwball*, 31.

8. Bogdanovich, *Who the Devil Made It*, 83.

9. Adela Rogers St. Johns, "A Gallant Lady . . . Carole Lombard," part one, *Liberty* (28 February 1942): 22.

10. Ibid.

11. Swindell, *Screwball*, 76.

12. Wes D. Gehring, "The Last William Wellman Interview," *Paper Cinema* 1, no. 1 (1982): 13.

13. Frank E. Vandiver, "Biography as an Agent of Humanism," in Stephen B. Oates, ed., *Biography as High Adventure: Life-writers Speak on Their Art* (Amherst: University of Massachusetts Press, 1986), 61.

14. See especially Carl Van Doren's, "The Revolt from the Village," *The Nation*, 12 October 1921, p. 407.

15. Glen A. Love, *Babbitt: An American Life* (New York: Twayne Publishers, 1993), 42.

16. See Wes D. Gehring, *Charlie Chaplin: A Bio-Bibliography* (Westport, Conn.: Greenwood Press, 1983), 9, 29.

17. David Robinson, *Chaplin: His Life and Art* (New York: McGraw-Hill, 1985), 352.

18. Frank "Kin" Hubbard, *Abe Martin, the Joker on Facts* (Indianapolis: Abe Martin Publishing Co., 1920), 64.

19. Will Rogers, "We Save Money, Egypt Loses It," 14 December 1924 syndicated weekly newspaper article, in James M. Smallwood, ed., *Will Rogers' Weekly Articles*, vol. 1, *The Harding/Coolidge Years: 1922–1925* (Stillwater: Oklahoma State University Press, 1980), 333–34.

Chapter 2

1. Frederick Russell, "The Life Story of Carole Lombard," part two, *Film Pictorial* (4 July 1936): 16.

2. Kyle Crichton, "Fun in Flickers," *Colliers* (24 February 1940): 11.

3. See Larry Swindell, *Screwball: The Life of Carole Lombard* (New York: William Morrow and Co., 1975), 40.

4. Crichton, "Fun in Flickers," 11.

5. Russell, "Life Story of Carole Lombard," part two, 17.

6. Adela Rogers St. Johns, "A Gallant Lady . . . Carole Lombard," part two, *Liberty* (7 March 1942): 25.

7. William Zinsser, ed., *Extraordinary Lives: The Art and Craft of American Biography* (Boston: Houghton Mifflin Co., 1986), 13.

8. Frederick Russell, "The Life Story of Carole Lombard," part one, *Film Pictorial* (27 June 1936): 10.

9. Adele Whitely Fletcher, "How Clark Gable and Carole Lombard Live," *Photoplay* (October 1940): 32.

10. Crichton, "Fun in Flickers," 11.

11. Ibid.

12. For example, this is the position taken in Russell, "Life Story of Carole Lombard," and Crichton, "Fun in Flickers," cited above.

13. Garson Kanin, *Hollywood* (New York: Viking Press, 1974), 63.

14. Swindell, *Screwball*, 51.

15. Adela Rogers St. Johns, "A Gallant Lady . . . Carole Lombard," part one, *Liberty* (28 February 1942): 23.

16. Homer Dickens, "Carole Lombard: Her Comic Sense Derived from an Instinctual Realism," *Films in Review* 12, no. 2 (February 1961): 71.

17. David McCullough, "The Unexpected Harry Truman," in Zinsser, ed., *Extraordinary Lives*, 57–58.

18. St. Johns, "A Gallant Lady . . . Carole Lombard," part one, 23.

19. Muriel Babcock, "Star Courage," *Silver Screen* (June 1937): 52–53, 76.

20. Virginia Wood, "Luck—and Lombard," *Screenland* (July 1937): 22.

21. St. Johns, "A Gallant Lady . . . Carole Lombard," part two, 28.

22. Maria DiBattista, *Fast-Talking Dames* (New Haven: Yale University Press, 2001), 113.

23. Wood, "Luck—and Lombard," 85.

24. Russell, "Life Story of Carole Lombard," part two, 17.

25. Ibid.

26. Mack Sennett and Cameron Ship, *King of Comedy* (1954;

reprint, New York: Pinnacle Books, 1975), 167.

27. Frederick W. Ott, *The Films of Carole Lombard* (1972; reprint, Secaucus, N.J.: Citadel Press, 1974), 19.

28. Ibid., 20.

29. Crichton, "Fun in Flickers," 39.

30. Gladys Hall, "Lombard—As She Sees Herself," *Motion Picture* (November 1938): 34–35, 66, 68.

31. Crichton, "Fun in Flickers," 39.

Chapter 3

1. Review of *Power* (Pathé), *Variety*, 28 November 1928.

2. Review of *Show Folks* (Pathé), *Picture Play* (March 1929).

3. Robert D. Matzen, *Carole Lombard: A Bio-Bibliography* (Westport, Conn.: Greenwood Press, 1988), 9.

4. Leonard Maltin, *Carole Lombard* (New York: Pyramid Publications, 1976), 26.

5. Review of *Ned McCobb's Daughter* (Pathé), *Film Spectator*, 10 November 1928.

6. Mordaunt Hall, "Sidney Howard's Play," review of *Ned McCobb's Daughter*, *New York Times*, 18 February 1929.

7. Maltin, *Carole Lombard*, 26.

8. Garson Kanin, *Hollywood* (New York: Viking Press, 1974), 59.

9. Carole Lombard, "Every Actor Should Take at Least One Week's Whirl at Publicity," *Hollywood Reporter* (24 October 1938).

10. Doris Kearns, "Angles of Vision," in *Telling Lives: The Biographer's Art*, Marc Pachter, ed. (1979; reprint, Philadelphia: University of Pennsylvania Press, 1985), 90–103.

11. Mordaunt Hall, "The Way of the Transgressor," review of *Me, Gangster* (Fox), *New York Times*, 22 October 1928.

12. Mordaunt Hall, "Newspaper Life in Film," review of *Big News* (Pathé), *New York Times*, 7 October 1929.

13. Carole Lombard, "My Man Gregory," *Screenbook* (February 1937): 38.

14. Ibid., 90.

15. *New York Times*, 7 October 1929.

16. Janet Bentley, "She Gets Away with Murder," *Photoplay* (March 1938): 27, 88–89.

17. Adela Rogers St. Johns, "A Gallant Lady . . . Carole Lombard," part two, *Liberty* (7 March 1942): 25.

18. Adele Whitely Fletcher, "How Clark Gable and Carole Lombard Live," *Photoplay* (October 1940): 31.

19. Frederick Russell, "The Life Story of Carole Lombard," part one, *Film Pictorial* (27 June 1936): 10.

20. Review of *Hearts and Spurs* (Fox), *Variety*, 15 July 1925.

21. Review of *The Arizona Kid* (Fox), *New York Times*, 17 May 1930.

22. Larry Swindell, *Screwball: The Life of Carole Lombard* (New York: William Morrow and Co., 1975), 86.

23. Russell, "The Life Story of Carole Lombard," part two, *Film Pictorial* (4 July 1936): 17.

24. For example, this is the case with film scholar Dave Smith's otherwise charming article, "Carole Lombard: Profane Angel," *Films of the Golden Age* (summer 2001): 20–38.

25. Review of *The Racketeer* (Fox), *Film Daily*, 12 January 1930.

26. Vivian Crates Logan, "Carol Lombard Converses as Easily as She Acts," *Fort Wayne News-Sentinel*, 18 June 1930.

27. Ibid.

28. Ibid.

29. *Redemption* theater advertisement, *Fort Wayne News-Sentinel*, 18 June 1930.

30. "Clara Bow Says Latest 'Boy Friend' Expensive," *Fort Wayne News-Sentinel*, 18 June 1930.

31. Logan, "Carol Lombard Converses as Easily as She Acts."

32. "Chuck Klein Back Amid Old Scenes," *Fort Wayne Journal-Gazette*, 18 June 1930.

33. Society column, *Fort Wayne Journal-Gazette*, 19 June 1930.

34. Logan, "Carol Lombard Converses as Easily as She Acts."

35. "Mrs. Alice Cheney Knight Succumbs in California," *Fort Wayne News-Sentinel*, 27 January 1930.

36. Swindell, *Carole Lombard,* 97.

37. Logan, "Carol Lombard Converses as Easily as She Acts."

Chapter 4

1. "Snappy Romances Head New Talkie Offerings," *Fort Wayne*

News-Sentinel, 21 June 1930.

2. *Safety in Numbers* Palace Theatre advertisement, ibid., 23 June 1930.

3. Review of *Safety in Numbers* (Paramount), *New York Daily News*, 31 May 1930.

4. Review of *Safety in Numbers*, *Variety*, 4 June 1930, and Robert Hage, review of *Safety in Numbers*, *Motion Picture Herald*, 7 June 1930.

5. Vivian Crates Logan, "Carol Lombard Converses as Easily as She Acts," *Fort Wayne News-Sentinel*, 18 June 1930.

6. Larry Swindell, *Screwball: The Life of Carole Lombard* (New York: William Morrow and Co., 1975), 87.

7. Logan, "Carol Lombard Converses as Easily as She Acts."

8. Homer Dickens, "Carole Lombard: Her Comic Sense Derived from an Instinctual Realism," *Films in Review* 12, no. 2 (February 1961): 73.

9. Swindell, *Screwball*, 98.

10. Garson Kanin, *Hollywood* (New York: Viking Press, 1974), 58.

11. Review of *Fast and Loose* (Paramount), *Motion Picture* (March 1931).

12. Leonard Maltin, *Carole Lombard* (New York: Pyramid Publications, 1976), 33.

13. Gerald Weales, *Canned Goods as Caviar: American Film Comedy of the 1930s* (Chicago: University of Chicago Press, 1985), 1.

14. Review of *It Pays to Advertise* (Paramount), *Variety*, 25 February 1931.

15. Robert D. Matzen, *Carole Lombard: A Bio-Bibliography* (Westport, Conn.: Greenwood Press, 1988), 11.

16. Ruth Biery, "Hollywood's Newest Romance," *Photoplay* (June 1931): 49.

17. Ibid., 106.

18. Ruth Biery, "Why Carole Changed Her Mind," *Photoplay* (September 1931): 55.

19. Michael Chabon, *Wonder Boys* (New York: Picador, 1995), 251.

20. David L. Smith, "Carole Lombard: Profane Angel," *Films of the Golden Age* (summer 2001): 30.

21. Gladys Hall, "There Are 7 Kinds of Love," *Photoplay*

(October 1933): 100.

22. Ibid.

23. Charles Francisco, *Gentleman: The William Powell Story* (New York: St. Martin's Press, 1985), 96.

24. Biery, "Why Carole Changed Her Mind," 105.

25. Francisco, *Gentleman*, 109.

26. Swindell, *Screwball*, 108.

27. Ibid.

28. Kanin, *Hollywood*, 60.

29. Kate Cameron, "Gary Cooper Does Well in 'I Take This Woman,'" review of *I Take This Woman* (Paramount), *New York Daily News*, 13 June 1931.

30. Review of *I Take This Woman*, *Variety*, 16 June 1931.

31. Thornton Delehanty, review of *I Take This Woman*, *New York Evening Post*, 13 June 1931.

32. John S. Cohen Jr., "'I Take This Woman' from the story 'Lost Ecstasy,'" *New York Sun*, 13 June 1931, and Marguerite Tazelaar, review of *I Take This Woman*, *New York Herald Tribune*, 13 June 1931.

33. Maltin, *Carole Lombard*, 42.

34. Gladys Hall, "Why I Married Bill Powell," *Motion Picture* (December 1931): 58–59, 99.

35. Elizabeth Goldbeck, "Bill Powell Talks about His Wife," *Movie Classic* (November 1932): 15, 68.

36. Louella D. Parsons, "Carole Gives Up Powell to Keep Career," 31 July 1933, Carole Lombard File, Margaret Herrick Library, Academy of Motion Picture Arts and Sciences, Beverly Hills, Calif.

37. Ibid.

38. Frederick Russell, "The Life Story of Carole Lombard," part two, *Film Pictorial* (4 July 1936): 25.

39. Ibid.

40. Uncredited source, 25 September 1933, Lombard File, Herrick library.

41. For example, see Jean Farge Guignol, "Intimate History of Carole Lombard," *Movie Mirror* (October 1937): 45.

Chapter 5

1. "Gable in a Gable Role Makes for Entertainment," review of *No Man of Her Own* (Paramount), *New York American*, 31 December 1932.

2. Ibid.

3. Marguerite Tazelaar, review of *No Man of Her Own*, *New York Herald Tribune*, 31 December 1932.

4. "Romantic Gamblers," review of *No Man of Her Own*, *New York Times*, 31 December 1932.

5. Review of *No Man of Her Own*, *Photoplay* (March 1933).

6. Charles Francisco, *Gentleman: The William Powell Story* (New York: St. Martin's Press, 1985), 117.

7. *No Man of Her Own* review, *Variety*, 3 January 1933.

8. Leonard Maltin, *Carole Lombard* (New York: Pyramid Publications, 1976), 52.

9. Garson Kanin, *Hollywood* (New York: Viking Press, 1974), 61.

10. Larry Swindell, *The Last Hero: A Biography of Gary Cooper* (Garden City, N.Y.: Doubleday and Co., 1980), 154–55.

11. Gabe Essoe, *The Films of Clark Gable* (Secaucus, N.J.: Citadel Press, 1972), 89.

12. Ibid., 140.

13. "An Indolent Husband," review of *Brief Moment* (Columbia), *New York Times*, 30 September 1933.

14. Larry Swindell, *Screwball: The Life of Carole Lombard* (New York: William Morrow and Co., 1975), 119.

15. Richard Watts Jr., "'Supernatural'—Paramount," review of *Supernatural*, *New York Herald Tribune*, 22 April 1933.

16. Mordaunt Hall, review of *Supernatural*, *New York Times*, 22 April 1933.

17. Kate Cameron, "Paramount Picture Spook Melodrama," review of *Supernatural*, *New York Daily News*, 22 April 1933.

18. "Carole Lombard's Arm Torn by Chimpanzee," 1 September 1933, uncredited source, Carole Lombard File, Margaret Herrick Library, Academy of Motion Picture Arts and Sciences, Beverly Hills, Calif.

19. Robert D. Matzen, *Carole Lombard: A Bio-Bibliography* (Westport, Conn.: Greenwood Press, 1988), 14.

20. Lewis Yablonsky, *George Raft* (New York: McGraw-Hill, 1974), 95.

21. Ibid., 96.

22. Maltin, *Carole Lombard*, 64.

23. George Raft, "The Role I Liked Best . . .," *Saturday Evening Post*, 24 January 1948.

24. "Raft, Lombard Perfect Team," review of *Bolero* (Paramount), *Hollywood Reporter*, 7 February 1934.

25. "Cast Names Are a Cinch Big Draw," *Hollywood Reporter*, 10 April 1934.

26. Cobbett Steinberg, *Reel Facts: The Movie Book of Records* (New York: Vintage Books, 1978), 404.

27. Matzen, *Carole Lombard*, 88.

28. "Russ Columbo Slain as Match Fires Old Gun," *Chicago Tribune*, 3 September 1934.

29. "Gun Accident Proves Fatal to Columbo," *Fort Wayne News-Sentinel*, 3 September 1934.

30. "Sally Blane, Carole Lombard Mourn Young 'Troubadour,'" 3 September 1934, uncredited source, Lombard File, Herrick Library.

31. Francisco, *Gentleman*, 139.

32. Sonia Lee, "We Would Have Married—," *Movie Classic* (December 1934): 37, 66.

33. "Sally Blane, Carole Lombard Mourn Young 'Troubadour,'" Herrick Library.

34. "Singer Paid Last Honor," *Los Angeles Times*, 7 September 1934.

35. Matzen, *Carole Lombard*, 14.

36. Lee, "We Would Have Married—," 66.

37. "Russ Columbo Dies from Accidental Gun Wound," *Los Angeles Times*, 3 September 1934.

38. Charles Thompson, *Bing: The Authorized Biography* (New York: David McKay Co., 1976), 51.

Chapter 6

1. Robert D. Matzen, *Carole Lombard: A Bio-Bibliography* (Westport, Conn.: Greenwood Press, 1988), 91.

2. Norbert Lusk, "J. Barrymore Superlatively Funny in Film," review of *Twentieth Century* (Columbia), *Los Angeles Times*, 13 May 1934.

3. Regina Crewe, "John Barrymore in Hilarious Role at the Music Hall," review of *Twentieth Century*, *New York American*, 4 May 1934.

4. Todd McCarthy, *Howard Hawks: The Grey Fox of Hollywood* (New York: Grove Press, 1997), 201.

5. Gerald Mast, *Howard Hawks, Storyteller* (New York: Oxford University Press, 1982), 194.

6. Ibid., 192.

7. McCarthy, *Howard Hawks*, 202.

8. Adela Rogers St. Johns, "A Gallant Lady . . . Carole Lombard," part two, *Liberty* (7 March 1942): 25.

9. Paramount press release for Carole Lombard, 4 March 1937, Carole Lombard File, Margaret Herrick Library, Academy of Motion Picture Arts and Sciences, Beverly Hills, Calif.

10. Jean Farge Guignol, "Intimate History of Carole Lombard," *Movie Mirror* (October 1937): 45.

11. Review of *Now and Forever* (Paramount), *Variety*, 16 October 1934.

12. Wanda Hale, "Carole Adopts Robson in Fan Dance Hilarity," review of *Lady by Choice* (Columbia), *New York Daily News*, 17 November 1934, and review of *Lady by Choice*, *Variety*, 20 November 1934.

13. Review of *Lady by Choice*, *New York Times*, 17 November 1934.

14. Review of *The Gay Bride* (MGM), *Variety*, 18 December 1934.

15. Andre Sennwald, review of *The Gay Bride*, *New York Times*, 19 December 1934, and Richard Watts Jr., "'The Gay Bride' of the Rackets," review of *The Gay Bride*, *New York Herald Tribune*, 19 December 1934.

16. Julie Lang Hunt, "How Carole Lombard Plans a Party," *Photoplay* (February 1935): 95.

17. Matzen, *Carole Lombard*, 17.

18. David Chierichetti, *Hollywood Director: The Career of Mitchell Leisen* (New York: Curtis Books, 1973), 94.

19. Ibid., 97.

20. Andre Sennwald, review of *Hands Across the Table* (Paramount), *New York Times*, 2 November 1935, and Rose Pelswick, "'Hands Across the Table': Diverting Light Comedy Stars Carole Lombard and Fred MacMurray," review of *Hands Across the Table*, *New York Evening Journal*, 2 November 1935.

21. Kate Cameron, "A Diverting Comedy at the Paramount," *New York Daily News*, 2 November 1935.

22. Eileen Creelman, "Some Gay Light Comedy in 'Hands Across the Table,' with Carole Lombard," review of *Hands Across the Table*, *New York Sun*, 2 November 1935.

23. For example, see John Reddington review of *Hands Across the Table*, *Brooklyn Daily Eagle*, 2 November 1935.

24. Beverly Hills, "Miss Lombard Scores in a Blithe New Comedy Romance," review of *Hands Across the Table*, *Liberty*, 23 November 1935.

25. Garson Kanin, *Hollywood* (New York: Viking Press, 1974), 61.

26. Ibid.

27. Edward Doherty, "Can the Gable-Lombard Love Story Have a Happy Ending?" *Photoplay* (May 1938): 77.

28. Kanin, *Hollywood*, 61.

Chapter 7

1. Noel F. Busch, "A Loud Cheer for the Screwball Girl," *Life*, 17 October 1938, p. 63.

2. Review of *The Princess Comes Across* (Paramount), *Variety*, 10 June 1936.

3. Regina Crewe, "'The Princess Comes Across' Is Delightful Film Offering with Its Humor and Thrills," review of *The Princess Comes Across*, *New York American*, 4 June 1934.

4. Howard Barnes, "'The Princess Comes Across'—Paramount," review of *The Princess Comes Across*, *New York Herald Tribune*, 4 June 1936.

5. Thornton Delehanty, "'The Princess Comes Across' Shown on Paramount Screen," review of *The Princess Comes Across*, *New York Post*, 4 June 1936.

6. Robert Lewis Taylor, *W. C. Fields: His Follies and Fortunes*

(New York: New American Library, 1967), 200.

7. Ibid., 201.

8. Pandro S. Berman, interview with author, June 1975, Hillcrest Country Club, Beverly Hills, Calif.

9. Carole Lombard, "My Man Gregory," *Screenbook* (February 1937): 38.

10. Ibid., 91.

11. Quentin Reynolds, "Give Me *Real* People," *Colliers* (26 March 1938): 53.

12. Ibid.

13. "'Godfrey' Role Keeps Carole Making Faces," *New York Post*, 12 September 1936.

14. Frank Nugent, review of *My Man Godfrey* (Universal), *New York Times*, 19 September 1936.

15. Howard Barnes, "'My Man Godfrey'—Music Hall," review of *My Man Godfrey*, *New York Herald Tribune*, 18 September 1936.

16. *My Man Godfrey* review, *Variety*, 23 September 1936.

17. Eileen Creelman, "The Music Hall Enjoys a Touch of Madness in Its Gay Comedy, 'My Man Godfrey,'" review of *My Man Godfrey*, *New York Sun*, 18 September 1936, and Rose Pelswick, "Amusing Dialogue and Slapstick Mark New Lombard-Powell Film Comedy," review of *My Man Godfrey*, *New York Evening Journal*, 18 September 1936.

18. "Powell, Lombard Farce Top Cinch Farce," *Hollywood Reporter*, 12 June 1936.

19. Kate Cameron, "Babies, Just Babies, On Music Hall Screen," review of *Bringing Up Baby* (RKO), *New York Daily News*, 4 March 1938.

20. Otis Ferguson, "While We Were Laughing," in *The Film Criticism of Otis Ferguson*, Robert Wilson, ed. (Philadelphia: Temple University Press, 1971), 24.

21. Leonard Maltin, *Carole Lombard* (New York: Pyramid Publications, 1976), 101.

22. See Kyle Crichton, "Fun in Flickers," *Colliers* (24 February 1940): 40.

23. Lyn Tornabene, *Long Live the King: A Biography of Clark Gable* (New York: G. P. Putnam's Sons, 1976), 201.

24. Ibid., 203.

25. "Actress Officially Carole Lombard Now," *Brooklyn Daily Eagle*, 6 November 1936.

26. "Fifty Best Draw Names," *Hollywood Reporter*, 27 July 1936.

27. Cobbett Steinberg, *Reel Facts: The Movie Book of Records* (New York: Vintage Books, 1978), 403–4.

28. See "Star Rating!" *New York Evening Journal*, 30 July 1936.

29. "Carole Lombard's Jewels for Sale," *New York Daily News*, 11 December 1936.

30. Frederick Lewis, "Is Carole Lombard in Love at Last?" *Liberty*, reissued 19 April 1975.

31. Kirtley Baskette, "Hollywood's Unmarried Husbands and Wives," *Photoplay* (January 1939): 22–23, 74.

32. Charles Samuels, *The King: A Biography of Clark Gable* (New York: Coward-McCann, 1962), 203.

Chapter 8

1. Archer Winsten, "'Swing High, Swing Low' at Paramount Theatre," review of *Swing High, Swing Low* (Paramount), *New York Post*, 15 April 1937.

2. Robert Garland, "Zestful Spring Tonic Is 'Swing High, Swing Low' Movie Musical," review of *Swing High, Swing Low*, *New York American*, 15 April 1937.

3. David Chierichetti, *Hollywood Director: The Career of Mitchell Leisen* (New York: Curtis Books, 1973), 110.

4. John Lahr, "Bring Me Sunshine," *The New Yorker*, 21 January 2002, p. 84.

5. Review of *My Man Godfrey* (Universal), *Variety*, 23 September 1936.

6. Chierichetti, *Hollywood Director*, 110.

7. Rose Pelswick, "Burlesque Theatre in Background of Lombard-MacMurray Musicale," *New York Evening Journal*, 15 April 1937.

8. Chierichetti, *Hollywood Director*, 113.

9. Anthony Quinn, *The Original Sin: A Self-Portrait* (Boston: Little, Brown and Co., 1972), 281–82.

10. James Harvey, *Romantic Comedy in Hollywood: From Lubitsch*

to Sturges (1987; reprint, New York: Da Capo Press, 1998), 204.

11. Wes D. Gehring, "The Last William Wellman Interview," *Paper Cinema* 1, no. 1 (1982): 13.

12. Regina Crewe, "'Nothing Sacred' Is Fast and Frisky Farce," review of *Nothing Sacred* (Selznick-International), *New York Journal American*, 26 November 1937.

13. Review of *Nothing Sacred*, *Variety*, 1 December 1937.

14. Kate Cameron, "'Nothing Sacred' Is a Riotous Comedy," review of *Nothing Sacred*, *New York Daily News*, 26 November 1937.

15. Review quoted in "Scripps-Howard Critics Select 'Nothing Sacred' for November," *New York World-Telegram*, 10 December 1937, *Nothing Sacred* File, Billy Rose Theatre Arts Collection, New York Public Library at Lincoln Center, New York, N.Y.

16. "Movie of the Week: *Nothing Sacred*," *Life*, 6 December 1937, p. 39.

17. Feg Murray, "Seein' Stars" (syndicated pictorial feature), *Fort Wayne Journal-Gazette*, 17 December 1937.

18. Frank S. Nugent, "A CHRISTMAS CAROLE: Being a Tardy Salute to Miss Lombard, One of Our Brightest Comediennes," *New York Times*, 19 December 1937.

19. Frank S. Nugent review of *True Confession* (Paramount), *New York Times*, 16 December 1937.

20. Bland Johaneson, "'True Confession': Top-Rank Comedians Support Leads," *New York Daily Mirror*, 16 December 1937, *True Confession* File, Rose Theatre Arts Collection.

21. Kate Cameron, "'True Confession' a Mad, Merry Farce," review of *True Confession*, *New York Daily News*, 16 December 1937.

22. Howard Barnes, "'True Confession'—Paramount," review of *True Confession*, *New York Herald Tribune*, 16 December 1937, and William Boehnel, "Law Given Some Digs in 'True Confession,'" review of *True Confession*, *New York World-Telegram*, 16 December 1937, *True Confession* File, Rose Theatre Arts Collection.

23. Review of *True Confession*, *Time*, 27 December 1937.

24. Ibid.

25. "Carole Lombard Plaque Dedication Set for January 1," *Fort Wayne News-Sentinel*, 10 December 1937.

26. "Plaque Designating Birthplace of Film Star Carole Lombard

to Be Dedicated Here Saturday," *Fort Wayne Journal-Gazette*, 30 December 1937.

27. For example, see Larry Swindell, *Screwball: The Life of Carole Lombard* (New York: William Morrow and Co., 1975), 232.

28. "Carole Lombard Views Plaque" (photograph and short text), *Fort Wayne Journal-Gazette*, 16 January 1938.

29. "Lombard Plaque Dedication Here This Afternoon," *Fort Wayne News-Sentinel*, 1 January 1938.

30. "Fake Relative Here Attempts to Victimize Carole Lombard," *Fort Wayne News-Sentinel*, 23 December 1937.

31. "Noted Comic Is Slightly Irked by Film Awards," *Washington Post*, 12 March 1937.

Chapter 9

1. Noel F. Busch, "A Loud Cheer for the Screwball Girl," *Life*, 17 October 1939, pp. 48, 50.

2. Garson Kanin, *Hollywood* (New York: Viking Press, 1974), 60.

3. Review of *Fools for Scandal* (Warner Brothers), *New York Times*, 25 May 1938.

4. Howard Barnes, "'Fools for Scandal'—Music Hall," review of *Fools for Scandal*, *New York Herald Tribune*, 25 March 1938.

5. Review of *Fools for Scandal*, *Variety*, 30 March 1938.

6. Wanda Hale, "'Fools for Scandal' Another Goofy Movie," review of *Fools for Scandal*, *New York Daily News*, 25 March 1938.

7. Robert D. Matzen, *Carole Lombard: A Bio-Bibliography* (Westport, Conn.: Greenwood Press, 1988), 25.

8. Busch, "Loud Cheer for the Screwball Girl," 48–51, 62–64.

9. Lyn Tornabene, *Long Live the King: A Biography of Clark Gable* (New York: G. P. Putnam's Sons, 1976), 212.

10. Rudy Behlmer, ed., *Memo from David O. Selznick: The Golden Years at Twentieth Century-Fox* (New York: New Grove Press, 1993).

11. Larry Swindell, *The Last Hero: A Biography of Gary Cooper* (Garden City, N.Y.: Doubleday and Co., 1980), 209.

12. Ibid., 210.

13. Charles Samuels, *The King: A Biography of Clark Gable* (New York: Coward-McCann, 1962), 231.

14. Ibid., 230.

15. Rose Pelswick, "'Made for Each Other' Story of Real Folk," review of *Made for Each Other* (Selznick-International), *New York Journal American*, 17 February 1939.

16. William Boehnel, "'Made for Each Other' Splendid," review of *Made for Each Other*, *New York World-Telegram*, 17 February 1939.

17. Review of *Made for Each Other*, *Variety*, 1 February 1939.

18. Cobbett Steinberg, *Reel Facts: The Movie Book of Records* (New York: Vintage Books, 1978), 312.

19. Larry Swindell, *Screwball: The Life of Carole Lombard* (New York: William Morrow and Co., 1975), 244.

20. Carole Lombard, "The Observation Post," *New York Daily News*, 28 February 1939.

21. Kirtley Baskette, "Hollywood's Unmarried Husbands and Wives," *Photoplay* (January 1939): 22–23, 74.

22. "Clark, Carole Go to Arizona for Wedding," *Fort Wayne News-Sentinel*, 30 March 1939.

23. Ibid.

24. See "Clark Gable and Carole Lombard Wed by Minister in an Arizona Ceremony," *New York Times*, 30 March 1939.

25. Review of *In Name Only* (RKO), *Variety*, 9 August 1939.

26. Review of *In Name Only*, *New York Times*, 4 August 1939.

27. "'In Name Only'—Music Hall," review of *In Name Only*, *New York Herald Tribune*, 4 August 1939.

28. Eileen Creelman, review of *In Name Only*, *New York Sun*, 4 August 1939.

29. Tornabene, *Long Live the King*, 243.

30. Warren G. Harris, *Gable and Lombard* (New York: Simon and Schuster, 1974), 112.

31. Vern Haugland, "Carole Lombard Assuming Role of Farmer's Wife and She Rustles Eggs for Gable," *Fort Wayne Journal-Gazette*, 1 October 1939.

32. Tornabene, *Long Live the King*, 248.

Chapter 10

1. Warren G. Harris, *Gable and Lombard* (New York: Simon and Schuster, 1974), 136.

2. "'Vigil in the Night' Is Enormously Fascinating," review of *Vigil in the Night* (RKO), *New York World-Telegram*, 9 March 1940, and review of *Vigil in the Night*, *Variety*, 7 February 1940.

3. Archer Winsten, "'Vigil in the Night' at the Roxy Theatre," review of *Vigil in the Night*, *New York Post*, 9 March 1940.

4. Eileen Creelman, review of *Vigil in the Night*, *New York Sun*, 9 March 1940.

5. "Lombard and Laughton View Their New Film and Find It Exciting," *Life*, 30 September 1940, pp. 47–50.

6. Review of *They Knew What They Wanted* (RKO), *Variety*, 9 October 1940.

7. Howard Barnes, "'They Knew What They Wanted'—Music Hall," review of *They Knew What They Wanted*, *New York Herald Tribune*, 11 October 1940.

8. Rose Pelswick, "'They Knew What They Wanted' Opens," review of *They Knew What They Wanted*, *New York Journal American*, 11 October 1940.

9. David Niven, *Bring on the Empty Horses* (New York: G. P. Putnam's Sons, 1975), 40.

10. Harris, *Gable and Lombard*, 51.

11. Lyn Tornabene, *Long Live the King: A Biography of Clark Gable* (New York: G. P. Putnam's Sons, 1976), 236.

12. William Boehnel, "'Mr. and Mrs. Smith' Gleeful Comedy," review of *Mr. and Mrs. Smith* (RKO), *New York World-Telegram*, 21 February 1941.

13. Review of *Mr. and Mrs. Smith*, *Variety*, 22 January 1941.

14. Gene Tierney, "'Mr. and Mrs. Smith'—Music Hall," review of *Mr. and Mrs. Smith*, *New York Herald Tribune*, 21 February 1941.

15. Irene Thirer, "'Mr. and Mrs. Smith' Gay Comedy at Music Hall," review of *Mr. and Mrs. Smith*, *New York Post*, 21 February 1941.

16. Boehnel, "'Mr. and Mrs. Smith' Gleeful Comedy."

17. Review of *Mr. and Mrs. Smith*, *New York Times*, 21 February 1941.

18. Kate Cameron, "New Hitchcock Film at the Music Hall," review of *Mr. and Mrs. Smith*, *New York Daily News*, 21 February 1941.

19. Frederick Othman, "Carole Lombard Gets Revenge by Directing Alfred Hitchcock," incomplete citation, Carole Lombard File, Margaret

Herrick Library, Academy of Motion Picture Arts and Sciences, Beverly Hills, Calif.

20. Ibid.

21. Tornabene, *Long Live the King*, 257.

22. Gladys Hall, "Lombard—As She Sees Herself," *Motion Picture* (November 1938): 34–35, 66, 68.

23. Scott Eyman, *Ernst Lubitsch: Laughter in Paradise* (New York: Simon and Schuster, 1993), 294.

24. "'To Be or Not to Be' Very Funny Anti-Nazi Comedy," review of *To Be or Not to Be* (United Artists), *Hollywood Reporter*, 18 February 1942.

25. Eyman, *Ernst Lubitsch*, 294.

26. Archer Winsten, "'To Be or Not to Be' Opens at the Rivoli Theatre," review of *To Be or Not to Be*, *New York Post*, 7 March 1942.

27. Leonard Maltin, *Carole Lombard* (New York: Pyramid Publications, 1976), 141.

Epilogue

1. Bosley Crowther, review of *To Be or Not to Be* (United Artists), *New York Times*, 22 March 1942.

2. Lee Mortimer, "'To Be or Not to Be' a Memorable Finale," review of *To Be or Not to Be*, *New York Mirror*, 7 March 1942.

3. "Farewell with a Laugh: Polish Actors Hamstring Nazis in Lombard's Last Comedy," *Newsweek*, 2 March 1942.

4. George Ross, "New Film at Rivoli Amusing," review of *To Be or Not to Be*, *New York World-Telegram*, 7 March 1942.

5. Conrad Lane, interview with author.

6. Noel F. Busch, "A Loud Cheer for the Screwball Girl," *Life*, 17 October 1938.

Select Bibliography

Books

Behlmer, Rudy, ed. *Memo from David O. Selznick: The Golden Years at Twentieth Century-Fox*. New York: Grove Press, 1993.

Bogdanovich, Peter. *Who the Devil Made It*. New York: Ballantine Books, 1997.

Chierichett, David. *Hollywood Director: The Career of Mitchell Leisen*. New York: Curtis Books, 1973.

DiBattista, Maria. *Fast-Talking Dames*. New Haven: Yale University Press, 2001.

Essoe, Gabe. *The Films of Clark Gable*. Secaucus, N.J.: Citadel Press, 1972.

Eyman, Scott. *Ernst Lubitsch: Laughter in Paradise*. New York: Simon and Schuster, 1993.

Ferguson, Otis. "While We Were Laughing." In *The Film Criticism of Otis Ferguson*, ed. Robert Wilson. Philadelphia: Temple University Press, 1971.

Francisco, Charles. *Gentleman: The William Powell Story*. New York: St. Martin's Press, 1985.

Gehring, Wes D. *American Dark Comedy: Beyond Satire*. Westport, Conn.: Greenwood Press, 1996.

———. *Charlie Chaplin: A Bio-Bibliography*. Westport, Conn.: Greenwood Press, 1983.

————. *Groucho and W. C. Fields: Huckster Comedians*. Jackson: University of Mississippi Press, 1994.

————. *Romantic Comedy versus Screwball Comedy: Charting a Difference*. Lanham, Md.: Scarecrow Press, 2002.

————. *Screwball Comedy: A Genre of Madcap Romance*. Westport, Conn.: Greenwood Press, 1986.

Harris, Warren G. *Gable and Lombard*. New York: Simon and Schuster, 1974.

Harvey, James. *Romantic Comedy in Hollywood: From Lubitsch to Sturges*. 1987. Reprint, New York: Da Capo Press, 1998.

Kanin, Garson. *Hollywood*. New York: Viking Press, 1974.

McCarthy, Todd. *Howard Hawks: The Grey Fox of Hollywood*. New York: Grove Press, 1997.

Maltin, Leonard. *Carole Lombard*. New York: Pyramid Publications, 1976.

Mast, Gerald. *Howard Hawks, Storyteller*. New York: Oxford University Press, 1982.

Matzen, Robert D. *Carole Lombard: A Bio-Bibliography*. Westport, Conn.: Greenwood Press, 1988.

Niven, David. *Bring on the Empty Horses*. New York: G. P. Putnam's Sons, 1975.

Ott, Frederick W. *The Films of Carole Lombard*. 1972. Reprint, Secaucus, N.J.: Citadel, 1974.

Quinn, Anthony. *The Original Sin: A Self-Portrait*. Boston: Little, Brown and Co., 1972.

Samuels, Charles. *The King: A Biography of Clark Gable*. New York: Coward-McCann, 1962.

Swindell, Larry. *The Last Hero: A Biography of Gary Cooper*. Garden City, N.Y.: Doubleday and Co., 1980.

————. *Screwball: The Life of Carole Lombard*. New York: William Morrow and Co., 1975.

Thompson, Charles. *Bing: The Authorized Biography*. New York: David McKay Co., 1976.

Tornabene, Lyn. *Long Live the King: A Biography of Clark Gable*. New York: G. P. Putnam's Sons, 1976.

Yablonsky, Lewis. *George Raft*. New York: McGraw-Hill, 1974.

Periodicals, manuscripts, and interviews

Babcock, Muriel. "Star Courage." *Silver Screen* (June 1937).

Baral, Robert. "Blonde Beauty Grows Up." *Photoplay* (May 1939).

Baskette, Kirtley. "Hollywood's Unmarried Husbands and Wives." *Photoplay* (January 1939).

Bentley, Janet. "She Gets Away with Murder." *Photoplay* (March 1938).

Berman, Pandro S. Interview with Wes Gehring. Beverly Hills, Calif., June 1975.

Biery, Ruth. "Hollywood's Newest Romance." *Photoplay* (June 1931).

———. "Why Carole Changed Her Mind." *Photoplay* (September 1931).

Busch, Noel F. "A Loud Cheer for the Screwball Girl." *Life* (17 October 1938).

"Carole Lombard Dies in Crash after Aiding U.S. Defense Bond Campaign." *Life* (26 January 1942).

"Carole Lombard's Arm Torn by Chimpanzee." 1 September 1933, uncredited source. Carole Lombard File. Margaret Herrick Library. Academy of Motion Picture Arts and Sciences, Beverly Hills, California.

"Carole Lombard Tells: 'How I Live by a Man's Code.'" *Photoplay* (June 1937).

"CATASTROPHE: End of a Mission." *Time* (26 January 1942).

Crichton, Kyle. "Fun in Flickers." *Colliers* (24 February 1940).

Denby, David. "Pauline Kael." *The New Yorker* (17 September 2001).

Dickens, Homer. "Carole Lombard: Her Comic Sense Derived from an Instinctual Realism." *Films in Review* 12, no. 2 (February 1961).

Doherty, Edward. "Can the Gable-Lombard Love Story Have a Happy Ending?" *Photoplay* (May 1938).

"Farewell with a Laugh: Polish Actors Hamstring Nazis in Lombard's Last Comedy." *Newsweek* (2 March 1942).

Review of *Fast and Loose* (Paramount). *Motion Picture* (March 1931).

Fletcher, Adele Whitely. "How Clark Gable and Carole Lombard Live." *Photoplay* (October 1940).

Gehring, Wes D. "The Last William Wellman Interview." *Paper Cinema* 1, no. 1 (1982).

————. "Carole Lombard: The Actress." *Indianapolis Star Magazine* (14 October 1979).

————. "The Patriotic Last Days of Carole Lombard," *Traces of Indiana and Midwestern History* 14, no. 2 (spring 2002).

————. Interview with Conrad Lane.

Goldbeck, Elizabeth. "Bill Powell Talks about His Wife." *Movie Classic* (November 1932).

Guignol, Jean Farge. "Intimate History of Carole Lombard." *Movie Mirror* (October 1937).

Hage, Robert. Review of *Safety in Numbers* (Paramount). *Motion Picture Herald* (7 June 1930).

Hall, Gladys. "Lombard—As She Sees Herself." *Motion Picture* (November 1938).

————. "There Are 7 Kinds of Love." *Photoplay* (October 1933).

————. "Why I Married Bill Powell." *Motion Picture* (December 1931).

Hills, Beverly. "Miss Lombard Scores in a Blithe New Comedy Romance." Review of *Hands Across the Table* (Paramount). *Liberty Magazine* (23 November 1935).

Hunt, Julie Lang. "How Carole Lombard Plans a Party." *Photoplay* (February 1935).

Lahr, John. "Bring Me Sunshine." *The New Yorker* (21 January 2002).

Lee, Sonia. "We Would Have Married—." *Movie Classic* (December 1934).

Lombard, Carole. "My Man Gregory." *Screenbook* (February 1937).

"Lombard and Laughton View Their New Film and Find It Exciting." *Life* (30 September 1940).

"Movie of the Week: *Nothing Sacred*." *Life* (6 December 1937).

Review of *Ned McCobb's Daughter* (Pathé). *Film Spectator* (10 November 1928).

Review of *No Man of Her Own* (Paramount). *Photoplay* (March 1933).

Othman, Frederick. "Carole Lombard Gets Revenge by Directing Alfred Hitchcock." Incomplete citation. Carole Lombard File. Margaret Herrick Library. Academy of Motion Picture Arts and Sciences, Beverly Hills, Calif.

Review of *The Racketeer* (Pathé). *Film Daily* (12 January 1930).

Raft, George. "The Role I Liked Best . . . ." *Saturday Evening Post* (24 January 1948).

Reynolds, Quentin. "Give Me *Real* People." *Colliers* (26 March 1938).

Russell, Frederick. "The Life Story of Carole Lombard." Parts 1 and 2. *Film Pictorial* (27 June 1936); (4 July 1936).

St. Johns, Adela Rogers. "A Gallant Lady . . . Carole Lombard." Parts 1 and 2. *Liberty* (28 February 1942); (7 March 1942).

"Sally Blane, Carole Lombard Mourn Young 'Troubadour.'" 3 September 1934, uncredited source. Carole Lombard File. Margaret Herrick Library. Academy of Motion Picture Arts and Sciences, Beverly Hills, Calif.

"Scripps-Howard Critics 'Nothing Sacred' for November." *New York World-Telegram*, 10 December 1937. *Nothing Sacred* File. Billy Rose Theatre Collection. New York Public Library at Lincoln Center, New York, New York.

Review of *Show Folks* (Pathé). *Picture Play* (March 1929).

Smith, David L. "Carole Lombard: Profane Angel." *Films of the Golden Age* (summer 2001).

Review of *True Confession* (Paramount). *Time* (27 December 1937).

Wood, Virginia. "Luck—and Lombard." *Screenland* (July 1937).

Newspapers (see individual citations in Notes)

Brooklyn Daily Eagle, 1935, 1936.

Chicago Tribune, 1934, 1942.

Fort Wayne Journal-Gazette, 1930, 1937, 1938, 1939, 1942.

Fort Wayne News-Sentinel, 1930, 1934, 1935, 1937, 1938, 1939, 1942.

Hollywood Reporter, 1934, 1936, 1938, 1942.

Indianapolis News, 1942.

Indianapolis Star, 1942.

Los Angeles Times, 1934.

New York American, 1932, 1934, 1936, 1937.

New York Daily News, 1930, 1931, 1933, 1935, 1936, 1937, 1938, 1939, 1941.

New York Evening Journal, 1935, 1936, 1937.

New York Evening Post, 1931.

New York Herald Tribune, 1931, 1932, 1934, 1936, 1937, 1938, 1939, 1940, 1941.

New York Journal American, 1937, 1939, 1940.

New York Mirror, 1937, 1942.

New York Post, 1936, 1937, 1940, 1942.

New York Sun, 1931, 1935, 1936, 1939, 1940.

New York Times, 1928, 1929, 1930, 1932, 1933, 1934, 1935, 1936, 1937, 1938, 1939, 1940, 1941, 1942.

New York World-Telegram, 1937, 1939, 1940, 1941, 1942.

Variety, 1928, 1930, 1931, 1933, 1934, 1936, 1937, 1938, 1939, 1940, 1941.

Washington (D.C.) Post, 1937.